Diabetic Cookbook

Diabetic Cookbook for Newly Diagnosed Simple and Easy Recipes for Balanced Meals and a Healthy Life

TABLE OF CONTENTS

The information in the following pages is broadly considered a truthful and accurate account of facts and as such, any inattention, use, or misuse of the information in question by the reader will render any resulting actions solely under their purview. There are no scenarios in which the publisher or the original author of this work can be in any fashion deemed liable for any hardship or damages that may befall them after undertaking information described herein. Additionally, the information in the following pages is intended only for informational purposes and should thus be thought of as universal. As befitting its nature, it is presented without assurance regarding its prolonged validity or interim quality. Trademarks that are mentioned are done without written consent and can in no way be considered an endorsement from the trademark holder.

Introduction

Diabetes mellitus, commonly known just as diabetes, is a disease that affects our metabolism. The predominant characteristic of diabetes is an inability to create or utilize insulin, a hormone that moves sugar from our blood cells into the rest of our bodies' cells. This is crucial for us because we rely on that blood sugar to power our body and provide energy. High blood sugar, if left untreated, can lead to serious damage of our eyes, nerves, kidneys, and other major organs. There are two major types of diabetes, type 1 and type 2, with the latter being the most common of the two with over 90 percent of diabetics suffering from it (Centers for Disease Control and Prevention, 2019).

Ham and Egg Cups

Preparation Time: 10 Minutes
Cooking Time: 15 Minutes
Servings: 4
Ingredients
- 5 slices ham
- 4 tbsp. cheese
- 1,5 tbsp. cream
- 3 egg whites
- 1,5 tbsp. pepper (green)
- 1 tsp. salt
- pepper to taste

Directions
1. Preheat oven to 350 F.
2. Arrange each slice of thinly sliced ham into 4 muffin tin.
3. Put 1/4 of grated cheese into ham cup.
4. Mix eggs, cream, salt and pepper and divide it into 2 tins.
5. Bake in oven 15 Minutes; after baking, sprinkle with green onions.

If you want to keep your current shape, also pay attention to this dish.

Nutrition:

Calories 180 / Protein 13 g / Fat 13 g / Carbs 2 g

Cauliflower Rice with Chicken

Preparation Time: 15 Minutes

Cooking Time: 15 Minutes

Servings: 4

Ingredients

- 1/2 large cauliflower
- 3/4 cup cooked meat
- 1/2 bell pepper
- 1 carrot
- 2 ribs celery
- 1 tbsp. stir fry sauce (low carb)
- 1 tbsp. extra virgin olive oil
- Salt and pepper to taste

Directions

1. Chop cauliflower in a processor to "rice." Place in a bowl.
2. Properly chop all vegetables in a food processor into thin slices.
3. Add cauliflower and other plants to WOK with heated oil. Fry until all veggies are tender.
4. Add chopped meat and sauce to the wok and fry 10 Minutes.

Serve.

This dish is very mouth-watering!

Nutrition:

Calories 200 / Protein 10 g / Fat 12 g /Carbs 10 g

Turkey with Fried Eggs

Preparation Time: 10 Minutes

Cooking Time: 20 Minutes

Servings: 4

Ingredients

- 4 large potatoes
- 1 cooked turkey thigh
- 1 large onion (about 2 cups diced)
- butter
- Chile flakes
- 4 eggs
- salt to taste
- pepper to taste

Directions

1. Rub the cold boiled potatoes on the coarsest holes of a box grater. Dice the turkey.
2. Cook the onion in as much unsalted butter as you feel comfortable with until it's just fragrant and translucent.
3. Add the rubbed potatoes and a cup of diced cooked turkey, salt and pepper to taste, and cook 20 Minutes.

Top each with a fried egg. Yummy!

Nutrition:

Calories 170 / Protein 19 g / Fat 7 g / Carbs 6 g

Sweet Potato, Kale, and White Bean Stew

Preparation time: 15 minutes
Cooking time: 25 minutes
Servings: 4
Ingredients:

- 1 (15-ounce) can low-sodium cannellini beans, rinsed and drained, divided

- 1 tablespoon olive oil

- 1 medium onion, chopped

- 2 garlic cloves, minced

- 2 celery stalks, chopped

- 3 medium carrots, chopped

- 2 cups low-sodium vegetable broth

- 1 teaspoon apple cider vinegar

- 2 medium sweet potatoes (about 1¼ pounds)

- 2 cups chopped kale

- 1 cup shelled edamame

- ¼ cup quinoa

- 1 teaspoon dried thyme

- 1/2 teaspoon cayenne pepper

- 1/2 teaspoon salt

- ¼ teaspoon freshly ground black pepper

Directions:

1. Put half the beans into a blender and blend until smooth. Set aside.

2. In a large soup pot over medium heat, heat the oil. When the oil is shining, include the onion and garlic, and cook until the onion softens and the garlic is sweet, about 3 minutes. Add the celery and carrots, and continue cooking until the vegetables soften, about 5 minutes.

3. Add the broth, vinegar, sweet potatoes, unblended beans, kale, edamame, and quinoa, and bring the mixture to a boil. Reduce the heat and simmer until the vegetables soften, about 10 minutes.

4. Add the blended beans, thyme, cayenne, salt, and black pepper, increase the heat to medium-high, and bring the mixture to a boil. Reduce the heat and simmer, uncovered, until the flavors combine, about 5 minutes.

5. Into each of 4 containers, scoop 1¾ cups of stew.

Nutrition: calories: 373; total fat: 7g; saturated fat: 1g; protein: 15g; total carbs: 65g; fiber: 15g; sugar: 13g; sodium: 540mg

Slow Cooker Two-Bean Sloppy Joes

Preparation time: 10 minutes
Cooking time: 6 hours
Servings: 4
Ingredients:

- 1 (15-ounce) can low-sodium black beans

- 1 (15-ounce) can low-sodium pinto beans

- 1 (15-ounce) can no-salt-added diced tomatoes

- 1 medium green bell pepper, cored, seeded, and chopped

- 1 medium yellow onion, chopped

- ¼ cup low-sodium vegetable broth

- 2 garlic cloves, minced

- 2 servings (¼ cup) meal prep barbecue sauce or bottled barbecue sauce

- ¼ teaspoon salt

- ¼ teaspoon freshly ground black pepper

- 4 whole-wheat buns

Directions:

1. In a slow cooker, combine the black beans, pinto beans, diced tomatoes, bell pepper, onion, broth, garlic, meal prep barbecue sauce, salt,

and black pepper. Stir the ingredients, then cover and cook on low for 6 hours.

2. Into each of 4 containers, spoon 1¼ cups of sloppy joe mix. Serve with 1 whole-wheat bun.

3. Storage: place airtight containers in the refrigerator for up to 1 week. To freeze, place freezer-safe containers in the freezer for up to 2 months. To defrost, refrigerate overnight. To reheat individual portions, microwave uncovered on high for 2 to 21/2 minutes. Alternatively, reheat the entire dish in a saucepan on the stove top. Bring the sloppy joes to a boil, then reduce the heat and simmer until heated through, 10 to 15 minutes. Serve with a whole-wheat bun.

Nutrition: calories: 392; total fat: 3g; saturated fat: 0g; protein: 17g; total carbs: 79g; fiber: 19g; sugar: 15g; sodium: 759mg

Lighter Eggplant Parmesan

Preparation time: 15 minutes
Cooking time: 35 minutes
Servings: 4
Ingredients:

- Nonstick cooking spray

- 3 eggs, beaten

- 1 tablespoon dried parsley

- 2 teaspoons ground oregano

- 1/8 teaspoon freshly ground black pepper

- 1 cup panko bread crumbs, preferably whole-wheat

- 1 large eggplant (about 2 pounds)

- 5 servings (21/2 cups) chunky tomato sauce or jarred low-sodium tomato sauce

- 1 cup part-skim mozzarella cheese

- ¼ cup grated parmesan cheese

Directions:

1. Preheat the oven to 450f. Coat a baking sheet with cooking spray.

2. In a medium bowl, whisk together the eggs, parsley, oregano, and pepper.

3. Pour the panko into a separate medium bowl.

4. Slice the eggplant into ¼-inch-thick slices. Dip each slice of eggplant into the egg mixture, shaking off the excess. Then dredge both sides of the eggplant in the panko bread crumbs. Place the coated eggplant on the prepared baking sheet, leaving a 1/2-inch space between each slice.

5. Bake for about 15 minutes until soft and golden brown. Remove from the oven and set aside to slightly cool.

6. Pour 1/2 cup of chunky tomato sauce on the bottom of an 8-by-15-inch baking dish. Using a spatula or the back of a spoon spread the tomato sauce evenly. Place half the slices of cooked eggplant, slightly overlapping, in the dish, and top with 1 cup of chunky tomato sauce, 1/2 cup of mozzarella and 2 tablespoons of grated parmesan. Repeat the layer, ending with the cheese.

7. Bake uncovered for 20 minutes until the cheese is bubbling and slightly browned.

8. Remove from the oven and allow cooling for 15 minutes before dividing the eggplant equally into 4 separate containers.

Nutrition: calories: 333; total fat: 14g; saturated fat: 6g; protein: 20g; total carbs: 35g; fiber: 11g; sugar: 15g; sodium: 994mg

---

Coconut-Lentil Curry

Preparation time: 15 minutes
Cooking time: 35 minutes
Servings: 4
Ingredients:

- 1 tablespoon olive oil

- 1 medium yellow onion, chopped

- 1 garlic clove, minced

- 1 medium red bell pepper, diced

- 1 (15-ounce) can green or brown lentils, rinsed and drained

- 2 medium sweet potatoes, washed, peeled, and cut into bite-size chunks (about 1¼ pounds)

- 1 (15-ounce) can no-salt-added diced tomatoes

- 2 tablespoons tomato paste

- 4 teaspoons curry powder

- 1/8 teaspoon ground cloves

- 1 (15-ounce) can light coconut milk

- ¼ teaspoon salt

- 2 pieces whole-wheat naan bread, halved, or 4 slices crusty bread

Directions:

1. In a large saucepan over medium heat, heat the olive oil. When the oil is shimmering, add both

---

the onion and garlic and cook until the onion softens and the garlic is sweet, for about 3 minutes.

2. Add the bell pepper and continue cooking until it softens, about 5 minutes more. Add the lentils, sweet potatoes, tomatoes, tomato paste, curry powder, and cloves, and bring the mixture to a boil. Reduce the heat to medium-low, cover, and simmer until the potatoes are softened, about 20 minutes.

3. Add the coconut milk and salt, and return to a boil. Reduce the heat and simmer until the flavors combine, about 5 minutes.

4. Into each of 4 containers, spoon 2 cups of curry.

5. Enjoy each serving with half of a piece of naan bread or 1 slice of crusty bread.

Nutrition: calories: 559; total fat: 16g; saturated fat: 7g; protein: 16g; total carbs: 86g; fiber: 16g; sugar: 18g; sodium: 819mg

Stuffed Portobello with Cheese

Preparation time: 15 minutes
Cooking time: 25 minutes
Servings: 4
Ingredients:

- 4 Portobello mushroom caps

- 1 tablespoon olive oil

- 1/2 teaspoon salt, divided

- ¼ teaspoon freshly ground black pepper, divided

- 1 cup baby spinach, chopped

- 11/2 cups part-skim ricotta cheese

- 1/2 cup part-skim shredded mozzarella cheese

- ¼ cup grated parmesan cheese

- 1 garlic clove, minced

- 1 tablespoon dried parsley

- 2 teaspoons dried oregano

- 4 teaspoons unseasoned bread crumbs, divided

- 4 servings (4 cups) roasted broccoli with shallots

Directions:

1. Preheat the oven to 375f. Line a baking sheet with aluminum foil.

2. Brush the mushroom caps with the olive oil, and sprinkle with ¼ teaspoon salt and 1/8 teaspoon

pepper. Put the mushroom caps on the prepared baking sheet and bake until soft, about 12 minutes.

3. In a medium bowl, mix together the spinach, ricotta, mozzarella, parmesan, garlic, parsley, oregano, and the remaining ¼ teaspoon of salt and 1/8 teaspoon of pepper.

4. Spoon 1/2 cup of cheese mixture into each mushroom cap, and sprinkle each with 1 teaspoon of bread crumbs. Return the mushrooms to the oven for an additional 8 to 10 minutes until warmed through.

5. Remove from the oven and allow the mushrooms to cool for about 10 minutes before placing each in an individual container. Add 1 cup of roasted broccoli with shallots to each container.

Nutrition: calories: 419; total fat: 30g; saturated fat: 10g; protein: 23g; total carbs: 19g; fiber: 2g; sugar: 3g; sodium: 790mg

Lighter Shrimp Scampi

Preparation time: 15 minutes
Cooking time: 15 minutes
Servings: 4
Ingredients:

- 11/2 pounds large peeled and deveined shrimp

- ¼ teaspoon salt

- 1/8 teaspoon freshly ground black pepper

- 2 tablespoons olive oil

- 1 shallot, chopped

- 2 garlic cloves, minced

- ¼ cup cooking white wine

- Juice of 1/2 lemon (1 tablespoon)

- 1/2 teaspoon sriracha

- 2 tablespoons unsalted butter, at room temperature

- ¼ cup chopped fresh parsley

- 4 servings (6 cups) zucchini noodles with lemon vinaigrette

Directions:

1. Season the shrimp with the salt and pepper.

2. In a medium saucepan over medium heat, heat the oil. Add the shallot and garlic, and cook until the shallot softens and the garlic is fragrant,

about 3 minutes. Add the shrimp, cover, and cook until opaque, 2 to 3 minutes on each side. Using a slotted spoon, transfer the shrimp to a large plate.

3. Add the wine, lemon juice, and sriracha to the saucepan, and stir to combine. Bring the mixture to a boil, then reduce the heat and simmer until the liquid is reduced by about half, 3 minutes. Add the butter and stir until melted, about 3 minutes. Return the shrimp to the saucepan and toss to coat. Add the parsley and stir to combine.

4. Into each of 4 containers, place 11/2 cups of zucchini noodles with lemon vinaigrette, and top with ¾ cup of scampi.

Nutrition: calories: 364; total fat: 21g; saturated fat: 6g; protein: 37g; total carbs: 10g; fiber: 2g; sugar: 6g; sodium: 557mg

Maple-Mustard Salmon

Preparation time: 10 minutes, plus 30 minutes marinating time
Cooking time: 20 minutes
Servings: 4
Ingredients:

- Nonstick cooking spray

- 1/2 cup 100% maple syrup

- 2 tablespoons Dijon mustard

- ¼ teaspoon salt

- 4 (5-ounce) salmon fillets

- 4 servings (4 cups) roasted broccoli with shallots

- 4 servings (2 cups) parsleyed whole-wheat couscous

Directions:

1. Preheat the oven to 400f. Line a baking sheet with aluminum foil and coat with cooking spray.

2. In a medium bowl, whisk together the maple syrup, mustard, and salt until smooth.

3. Put the salmon fillets into the bowl and toss to coat. Cover and place in the refrigerator to marinate for at least 30 minutes and up to overnight.

4. Shake off excess marinade from the salmon fillets and place them on the prepared baking

---

sheet, leaving a 1-inch space between each fillet. Discard the extra marinade.

5. Bake for about 20 minutes until the salmon is opaque and a thermometer inserted in the thickest part of a fillet reads 145f.

6. Into each of 4 resealable containers, place 1 salmon fillet, 1 cup of roasted broccoli with shallots, and 1/2 cup of parsleyed whole-wheat couscous.

Nutrition: calories: 601; total fat: 29g; saturated fat: 4g; protein: 36g; total carbs: 51g; fiber: 3g; sugar: 23g; sodium: 610mg

Chicken Salad with Grapes and Pecans

Preparation Time: 15 Minutes
Cooking Time: 5 Minutes
Servings: 4
Ingredients:

- 1/3 cup unsalted pecans, chopped

- 10 ounces cooked skinless, boneless chicken breast or rotisserie chicken, finely chopped

- 1/2 medium yellow onion, finely chopped

- 1 celery stalk, finely chopped

- ¾ cup red or green seedless grapes, halved

- ¼ cup light mayonnaise

- ¼ cup nonfat plain Greek yogurt

- 1 tablespoon Dijon mustard

- 1 tablespoon dried parsley

- ¼ teaspoon salt

- 1/8 teaspoon freshly ground black pepper

- 1 cup shredded romaine lettuce

- 4 (8-inch) whole-wheat pitas

Directions:

1. Heat a small skillet over medium-low heat to toast the pecans. Cook the pecans until fragrant,

about 3 minutes. Remove from the heat and set aside to cool.

2. In a medium bowl, mix the chicken, onion, celery, pecans, and grapes.

3. In a small bowl, whisk together the mayonnaise, yogurt, mustard, parsley, salt, and pepper. Spoon the sauce over the chicken mixture and stir until well combined.

4. Into each of 4 containers, place ¼ cup of lettuce and top with 1 cup of chicken salad. Store the pitas separately until ready to serve.

5. When ready to eat, stuff the serving of salad and lettuce into 1 pita.

Nutrition: Calories: 418; Total Fat: 14g; Saturated Fat: 2g; Protein: 31g; Total Carbs: 43g; Fiber: 6g;

Roasted Vegetables

Preparation time: 14 minutes
Cooking time: 17 minutes
Servings: 3
Ingredients:

- 4 Tbsp. olive oil, reserve some for greasing

- 2 heads, large garlic, tops sliced off

- 2 large eggplants/aubergine, tops removed, cubed

- 2 large shallots, peeled, quartered

- 1 large carrot, peeled, cubed

- 1 large parsnips, peeled, cubed

- 1 small green bell pepper, deseeded, ribbed, cubed

- 1 small red bell pepper, deseeded, ribbed, cubed

- ½ pound Brussels sprouts, halved, do not remove cores

- 1 sprig, large thyme, leaves picked

- sea salt, coarse-grained

For garnish

- 1 large lemon, halved, ½ squeezed, ½ sliced into smaller wedges

- ⅛ cup fennel bulb, minced

Directions:

1. From 425°F or 220°C preheat oven for at least 5 minutes before using.

2. Line deep roasting pan with aluminum foil; lightly grease with oil. Tumble in bell peppers, Brussels sprouts, carrots, eggplants, garlic, parsnips, rosemary leaves, shallots, and thyme. Add a pinch of sea salt; drizzle in remaining oil and lemon juice. Toss well to combine.

3. Cover roasting pan with a sheet of aluminum foil. Place this on middle rack of oven. Bake for 20 to 30 minutes. Remove aluminum foil. Roast, for another 5 to 10 minutes, or until some vegetables brown at the edges. Remove roasting pan from oven. Cool slightly before ladling equal portions into plates.

4. Garnish with fennel and a wedge of lemon. Squeeze lemon juice on top of dish before eating.

Nutrition:
Calories 163
Total Fat 4.2 g
Saturated Fat 0.8 g
Cholesterol 0 mg
Sodium 861 mg
Total Carbs 22.5 g
Fiber 6.3 g
Sugar 2.3 g
Protein 9.2 g

Millet Pilaf

Preparation time: 10 minutes
Cooking time: 15 minutes
Servings: 4
Ingredients:

- 1 cup millet
- 2 tomatoes, rinsed, seeded, and chopped
- 1¾ cups filtered water
- 2 tablespoons extra-virgin olive oil
- ¼ cup chopped dried apricot
- Zest of 1 lemon
- Juice of 1 lemon
- ½ cup fresh parsley, rinsed and chopped
- Himalayan pink salt
- Freshly ground black pepper

Directions:

1. In an electric pressure cooker, combine the millet, tomatoes, and water. Lock the lid into place, select Manual and High Pressure, and cook for 7 minutes.

2. When the beep sounds, quick release the pressure by pressing Cancel and twisting the steam valve to the Venting position. Carefully remove the lid.

3. Stir in the olive oil, apricot, lemon zest, lemon juice, and parsley. Taste, season with salt and pepper, and serve.

Nutrition:

Calories: 270

Total fat: 8g

Total carbohydrates: 42g

Fiber: 5g

Sugar: 3g

Protein: 6g

Sweet and Sour Onions

Preparation time: 10 minutes
Cooking time: 11 minutes
Servings: 4
Ingredients:
- 4 large onions, halved
- 2 garlic cloves, crushed
- 3 cups vegetable stock
- 1 ½ tablespoon balsamic vinegar
- ½ teaspoon Dijon mustard
- 1 tablespoon sugar

Directions:
1. Combine onions and garlic in a pan. Fry for 3 minutes, or till softened.
2. Pour stock, vinegar, Dijon mustard, and sugar. Bring to a boil.
3. Reduce heat. Cover and let the combination simmer for 10 minutes.
4. Get rid of from heat. Continue stirring until the liquid is reduced and the onions are brown. Serve.

Nutrition:
Calories 203
Total Fat 41.2 g
Saturated Fat 0.8 g

Cholesterol 0 mg
Sodium 861 mg
Total Carbs 29.5 g
Fiber 16.3 g
Sugar 29.3 g
Protein 19.2 g

Sautéed Apples and Onions

Preparation time: 14 minutes
Cooking time: 16 minutes
Servings: 3
Ingredients:
- 2 cups dry cider

- 1 large onion, halved

- 2 cups vegetable stock

- 4 apples, sliced into wedges

- Pinch of salt

- Pinch of pepper

Directions:
1. Combine cider and onion in a saucepan. Bring to a boil until the onions are cooked and liquid almost gone.

2. Pour the stock and the apples. Season with salt and pepper. Stir occasionally. Cook for about 10 minutes or until the apples are tender but not mushy. Serve.

Nutrition:
Calories 343
Total Fat 51.2 g
Saturated Fat 0.8 g
Cholesterol 0 mg
Sodium 861 mg
Total Carbs 22.5 g

Fiber 6.3 g
Sugar 2.3 g
Protein 9.2 g

Zucchini Noodles with Portabella Mushrooms

Preparation time: 14 minutes
Cooking time: 16 minutes
Servings: 3
Ingredients:

- 1 zucchini, processed into spaghetti-like noodles

- 3 garlic cloves, minced

- 2 white onions, thinly sliced

- 1 thumb-sized ginger, julienned

- 1 lb. chicken thighs

- 1 lb. portabella mushrooms, sliced into thick slivers

- 2 cups chicken stock

- 3 cups water

- Pinch of sea salt, add more if needed

- Pinch of black pepper, add more if needed

- 2 tsp. sesame oil

- 4 Tbsp. coconut oil, divided

- ¼ cup fresh chives, minced, for garnish

Directions:
1. Pour 2 tablespoons of coconut oil into a large saucepan. Fry mushroom slivers in batches for 5

minutes or until seared brown. Set aside. Transfer these to a plate.

2. Sauté the onion, garlic, and ginger for 3 minutes or until tender. Add in chicken thighs, cooked mushrooms, chicken stock, water, salt, and pepper stir mixture well. Bring to a boil.

3. Decrease gradually the heat and allow simmering for 20 minutes or until the chicken is forking tender. Tip in sesame oil.

4. Serve by placing an equal amount of zucchini noodles into bowls. Ladle soup and garnish with chives.

Nutrition:
Calories 163
Total Fat 4.2 g
Saturated Fat 0.8 g
Cholesterol 0 mg
Sodium 861 mg
Total Carbs 22.5 g
Fiber 6.3 g
Sugar 2.3 g
Protein 9.2 g

Grilled Tempeh with Pineapple

Preparation time: 12 minutes
Cooking time: 16 minutes
Servings: 3
Ingredients:

- 10 oz. tempeh, sliced

- 1 red bell pepper, quartered

- 1/4 pineapple, sliced into rings

- 6 oz. green beans

- 1 tbsp. coconut aminos

- 2 1/2 tbsp. orange juice, freshly squeeze

- 1 1/2 tbsp. lemon juice, freshly squeezed

- 1 tbsp. extra virgin olive oil

- 1/4 cup hoisin sauce

Directions:

1. Blend together the olive oil, orange and lemon juices, coconut aminos or soy sauce, and hoisin sauce in a bowl. Add the diced tempeh and set aside.

2. Heat up the grill or place a grill pan over medium high flame. Once hot, lift the marinated tempeh from the bowl with a pair of tongs and transfer them to the grill or pan.

3. Grille for 2 to 3 minutes, or until browned all over.

4. Grill the sliced pineapples alongside the tempeh, then transfer them directly onto the serving platter.

5. Place the grilled tempeh beside the grilled pineapple and cover with aluminum foil to keep warm.

6. Meanwhile, place the green beans and bell peppers in a bowl and add just enough of the marinade to coat.

7. Prepare the grill pan and add the vegetables. Grill until fork tender and slightly charred.

8. Transfer the grilled vegetables to the serving platter and arrange artfully with the tempeh and pineapple. Serve at once.

Nutrition:
Calories 163
Total Fat 4.2 g
Saturated Fat 0.8 g
Cholesterol 0 mg
Sodium 861 mg
Total Carbs 22.5 g
Fiber 6.3 g
Sugar 2.3 g
Protein 9.2 g

Courgettes In Cider Sauce

Preparation time: 13 minutes
Cooking time: 17 minutes
Servings: 3
Ingredients:
- 2 cups baby courgettes

- 3 tablespoons vegetable stock

- 2 tablespoons apple cider vinegar

- 1 tablespoon light brown sugar

- 4 spring onions, finely sliced

- 1 piece fresh gingerroot, grated

- 1 teaspoon corn flour

- 2 teaspoons water

Directions:
1. Bring a pan with salted water to a boil. Add courgettes. Bring to a boil for 5 minutes.

2. Meanwhile, in a pan, combine vegetable stock, apple cider vinegar, brown sugar, onions, gingerroot, lemon juice and rind, and orange juice and rind. Take to a boil. Lower the heat and allow simmering for 3 minutes.

3. Mix the corn flour with water. Stir well. Pour into the sauce. Continue stirring until the sauce thickens.

4. Drain courgettes. Transfer to the serving dish. Spoon over the sauce. Toss to coat courgettes. Serve.

Nutrition:

Calories 173

Total Fat 9.2 g

Saturated Fat 0.8 g

Cholesterol 0 mg

Sodium 861 mg

Total Carbs 22.5 g

Fiber 6.3 g

Sugar 2.3 g

Protein 9.2 g

Baked Mixed Mushrooms

Preparation time: 8 minutes
Cooking time: 20 minutes
Servings: 3
Ingredients:

- 2 cups mixed wild mushrooms

- 1 cup chestnut mushrooms

- 2 cups dried porcini

- 2 shallots

- 4 garlic cloves

- 3 cups raw pecans

- ½ bunch fresh thyme

- 1 bunch flat-leaf parsley

- 2 tablespoons olive oil

- 2 fresh bay leaves

- 1 ½ cups stale bread

Directions:

1. Remove skin and finely chop garlic and shallots. Roughly chop the wild mushrooms and chestnut mushrooms. Pick the leaves of the thyme and tear the bread into small pieces. Put inside the pressure cooker.

2. Place the pecans and roughly chop the nuts. Pick the parsley leaves and roughly chop.

---

3. Place the porcini in a bowl then add 300ml of boiling water. Set aside until needed.

4. Heat oil in the pressure cooker. Add the garlic and shallots. Cook for 3 minutes while stirring occasionally.

5. Drain porcini and reserve the liquid. Add the porcini into the pressure cooker together with the wild mushrooms and chestnut mushrooms. Add the bay leaves and thyme.

6. Position the lid and lock in place. Put to high heat and bring to high pressure. Adjust heat to stabilize. Cook for 10 minutes. Adjust taste if necessary.

7. Transfer the mushroom mixture into a bowl and set aside to cool completely.

8. Once the mushrooms are completely cool, add the bread, pecans, a pinch of black pepper and sea salt, and half of the reserved liquid into the bowl. Mix well. Add more reserved liquid if the mixture seems dry.

9. Add more than half of the parsley into the bowl and stir. Transfer the mixture into a 20cm x 25cm lightly greased baking dish and cover with tin foil.

10. Bake in the oven for 35 minutes. Then, get rid of the foil and cook for another 10 minutes. Once done, sprinkle the remaining

parsley on top and serve with bread or crackers. Serve.

Nutrition:
Calories 343
Total Fat 4.2 g
Saturated Fat 0.8 g
Cholesterol 0 mg
Sodium 861 mg
Total Carbs 22.5 g
Fiber 6.3 g
Sugar 2.3 g
Protein 9.2 g

Spiced Okra

Preparation time: 14 minutes
Cooking time: 16 minutes
Servings: 3
Ingredients:

- 2 cups okra

- ¼ teaspoon stevia

- 1 teaspoon chilli powder

- ½ teaspoon ground turmeric

- 1 tablespoon ground coriander

- 2 tablespoons fresh coriander, chopped

- 1 tablespoon ground cumin

- ¼ teaspoon salt

- 1 tablespoon desiccated coconut

- 3 tablespoons vegetable oil

- ½ teaspoon black mustard seeds

- ½ teaspoon cumin seeds

- Fresh tomatoes, to garnish

Directions:

1. Trim okra. Wash and dry.

2. Combine stevia, chilli powder, turmeric, ground coriander, fresh coriander, cumin, salt, and desiccated coconut in a bowl.

3. Heat the oil in a pan. Cook mustard and cumin seeds for 3 minutes. Stir continuously. Add okra. Tip in the spice mixture. Cook on low heat for 8 minutes.

4. Transfer to a serving dish. Garnish with fresh tomatoes.

Nutrition:
Calories 163
Total Fat 4.2 g
Saturated Fat 0.8 g
Cholesterol 0 mg
Sodium 861 mg
Total Carbs 22.5 g
Fiber 6.3 g
Sugar 2.3 g
Protein 9.2 g

Dinner Recipes

Misto Quente

Preparation time: 5 minutes

Cooking time: 10 minutes

Servings: 4

Ingredients:

- 4 slices of bread without shell
- 4 slices of turkey breast
- 4 slices of cheese
- 2 tbsp. cream cheese
- 2 spoons of butter

Directions:

1. Preheat the air fryer. Set the timer of 5 minutes and the temperature to 200C.
2. Pass the butter on one side of the slice of bread, and on the other side of the slice, the cream cheese.
3. Mount the sandwiches placing two slices of turkey breast and two slices cheese between the breads, with the cream cheese inside and the side with butter.
4. Place the sandwiches in the basket of the air fryer. Set the timer of the air fryer for 5 minutes and press the power button.

Nutrition: Calories: 340 Fat: 15g Carbohydrates: 32g Protein: 15g Sugar: 0g Cholesterol: 0mg

Garlic Bread

Preparation time: 10 minutes

Cooking time: 15 minutes

Servings: 4-5

Ingredients:

- 2 stale French rolls
- 4 tbsp. crushed or crumpled garlic
- 1 cup of mayonnaise
- Powdered grated Parmesan
- 1 tbsp. olive oil

Directions:

1. Preheat the air fryer. Set the time of 5 minutes and the temperature to 2000C.
2. Mix mayonnaise with garlic and set aside.
3. Cut the baguettes into slices, but without separating them completely.
4. Fill the cavities of equals. Brush with olive oil and sprinkle with grated cheese.
5. Place in the basket of the air fryer. Set the timer to 10 minutes, adjust the temperature to 1800C and press the power button.

Nutrition: Calories: 340 Fat: 15g Carbohydrates: 32g Protein: 15g Sugar: 0g Cholesterol: 0mg

Bruschetta

Preparation time: 5 minutes
Cooking time: 10 minutes
Servings: 2
Ingredients:

- 4 slices of Italian bread
- 1 cup chopped tomato tea
- 1 cup grated mozzarella tea
- Olive oil
- Oregano, salt, and pepper
- 4 fresh basil leaves

Directions:

1. Preheat the air fryer. Set the timer of 5 minutes and the temperature to 2000C.
2. Sprinkle the slices of Italian bread with olive oil. Divide the chopped tomatoes and mozzarella between the slices. Season with salt, pepper, and oregano.
3. Put oil in the filling. Place a basil leaf on top of each slice.
4. Put the bruschetta in the basket of the air fryer being careful not to spill the filling. Set the timer of 5 minutes, set the temperature to 180C, and press the power button.
5. Transfer the bruschetta to a plate and serve.

Nutrition: Calories: 434 Fat: 14g Carbohydrates: 63g Protein: 11g Sugar: 8g Cholesterol: 0mg

Cream Buns with Strawberries

Preparation time: 10 minutes
Cooking time: 12 minutes
Servings: 6
Ingredients:

- 240g all-purpose flour
- 50g granulated sugar
- 8g baking powder
- 1g of salt
- 85g chopped cold butter
- 84g chopped fresh strawberries
- 120 ml whipping cream
- 2 large eggs
- 10 ml vanilla extract
- 5 ml of water

Directions:

1. Sift flour, sugar, baking powder and salt in a large bowl. Put the butter with the flour with the use of a blender or your hands until the mixture resembles thick crumbs.
2. Mix the strawberries in the flour mixture. Set aside for the mixture to stand. Beat the whipping cream, 1 egg and the vanilla extract in a separate bowl.
3. Put the cream mixture in the flour mixture until they are homogeneous, and then spread the mixture to a thickness of 38 mm.
4. Use a round cookie cutter to cut the buns. Spread the buns with a combination of egg and water. Set aside

5. Preheat the air fryer, set it to 180C.
6. Place baking paper in the preheated inner basket.
7. Place the buns on top of the baking paper and cook for 12 minutes at 180C, until golden brown.

Nutrition: Calories: 150Fat: 14g Carbohydrates: 3g Protein: 11g Sugar: 8g Cholesterol: 0mg

Blueberry Buns

Preparation time: 10 minutes

Cooking time: 12 minutes

Servings: 6

Ingredients:

- 240g all-purpose flour
- 50g granulated sugar
- 8g baking powder
- 2g of salt
- 85g chopped cold butter
- 85g of fresh blueberries
- 3g grated fresh ginger
- 113 ml whipping cream
- 2 large eggs
- 4 ml vanilla extract
- 5 ml of water

Directions:

1. Put sugar, flour, baking powder and salt in a large bowl.
2. Put the butter with the flour using a blender or your hands until the mixture resembles thick crumbs.
3. Mix the blueberries and ginger in the flour mixture and set aside
4. Mix the whipping cream, 1 egg and the vanilla extract in a different container.
5. Put the cream mixture with the flour mixture until combined.

6. Shape the dough until it reaches a thickness of approximately 38 mm and cut it into eighths.
7. Spread the buns with a combination of egg and water. Set aside Preheat the air fryer set it to 180C.
8. Place baking paper in the preheated inner basket and place the buns on top of the paper. Cook for 12 minutes at 180C, until golden brown

Nutrition: Calories: 105 Fat: 1.64g Carbohydrates: 20.09gProtein: 2.43g Sugar: 2.1g Cholesterol: 0mg

Cauliflower Potato Mash

Preparation Time: 30 minutes Servings: 4
Cooking Time: 5 minutes
Ingredients:

- 2 cups potatoes, peeled and cubed
- 2 tbsp. butter
- ¼ cup milk
- 10 oz. cauliflower florets
- ¾ tsp. salt

Directions:

1. Add water to the saucepan and bring to boil.
2. Reduce heat and simmer for 10 minutes.
3. Drain vegetables well. Transfer vegetables, butter, milk, and salt in a blender and blend until smooth.
4. Serve and enjoy.

Nutrition: Calories 128 Fat 6.2 g, Sugar 3.3 g, Protein 3.2 g, Cholesterol 17 mg

French toast in Sticks

Preparation time: 5 minutes
Cooking time: 10 minutes
Servings: 4
Ingredients:

- 4 slices of white bread, 38 mm thick, preferably hard
- 2 eggs
- 60 ml of milk
- 15 ml maple sauce
- 2 ml vanilla extract
- Nonstick Spray Oil
- 38g of sugar
- 3ground cinnamon
- Maple syrup, to serve
- Sugar to sprinkle

Directions:

1. Cut each slice of bread into thirds making 12 pieces. Place sideways
2. Beat the eggs, milk, maple syrup and vanilla.
3. Preheat the air fryer, set it to 175C.
4. Dip the sliced bread in the egg mixture and place it in the preheated air fryer. Sprinkle French toast generously with oil spray.
5. Cook French toast for 10 minutes at 175C. Turn the toast halfway through cooking.
6. Mix the sugar and cinnamon in a bowl.
7. Cover the French toast with the sugar and cinnamon mixture when you have finished cooking.

8. Serve with Maple syrup and sprinkle with powdered sugar

Nutrition: Calories 128 Fat 6.2 g, Carbohydrates 16.3 g, Sugar 3.3 g, Protein 3.2 g, Cholesterol 17 mg

Muffins Sandwich

Preparation time: 2 minutes

Cooking time: 10 minutes

Servings: 1

Ingredients:

- Nonstick Spray Oil
- 1 slice of white cheddar cheese
- 1 slice of Canadian bacon
- 1 English muffin, divided
- 15 ml hot water
- 1 large egg
- Salt and pepper to taste

Directions:

1. Spray the inside of an 85g mold with oil spray and place it in the air fryer.
2. Preheat the air fryer, set it to 160C.
3. Add the Canadian cheese and bacon in the preheated air fryer.
4. Pour the hot water and the egg into the hot pan and season with salt and pepper.
5. Select Bread, set to 10 minutes.
6. Take out the English muffins after 7 minutes, leaving the egg for the full time.
7. Build your sandwich by placing the cooked egg on top of the English muffing and serve

Nutrition: Calories 400 Fat 26g, Carbohydrates 26g, Sugar 15 g, Protein 3 g, Cholesterol 155 mg

Bacon BBQ

Preparation time: 2 minutes
Cooking time: 8 minutes
Servings: 2
Ingredients:

- 13g dark brown sugar
- 5g chili powder
- 1g ground cumin
- 1g cayenne pepper
- 4 slices of bacon, cut in half

Directions:

1. Mix seasonings until well combined.
2. Dip the bacon in the dressing until it is completely covered. Leave aside.
3. Preheat the air fryer, set it to 160C.
4. Place the bacon in the preheated air fryer
5. Select Bacon and press Start/Pause.

Nutrition: Calories: 1124 Fat: 72g Carbohydrates: 59g Protein: 49g Sugar: 11g Cholesterol: 77mg

Stuffed French toast

Preparation time: 4 minutes
Cooking time: 10 minutes
Servings: 1
Ingredients:

- 1 slice of brioche bread,
- 64 mm thick, preferably rancid
- 113g cream cheese
- 2 eggs
- 15 ml of milk
- 30 ml whipping cream
- 38g of sugar
- 3g cinnamon
- 2 ml vanilla extract
- Nonstick Spray Oil
- Pistachios chopped to cover
- Maple syrup, to serve

Directions:

1. Preheat the air fryer, set it to 175C.
2. Cut a slit in the middle of the muffin.
3. Fill the inside of the slit with cream cheese. Leave aside.
4. Mix the eggs, milk, whipping cream, sugar, cinnamon, and vanilla extract.
5. Moisten the stuffed French toast in the egg mixture for 10 seconds on each side.
6. Sprinkle each side of French toast with oil spray.
7. Place the French toast in the preheated air fryer and cook for 10 minutes at 175C

---

8. Stir the French toast carefully with a spatula when you finish cooking.
9. Serve topped with chopped pistachios and acrid syrup.

Nutrition: Calories: 159Fat: 7.5g Carbohydrates: 25.2g Protein: 14g Sugar: 0g Cholesterol: 90mg

Scallion Sandwich

Preparation Time: 10 minutes

Cooking Time: 10 minutes

Servings: 1

Ingredients:

- 2 slices wheat bread
- 2 teaspoons butter, low fat
- 2 scallions, sliced thinly
- 1 tablespoon of parmesan cheese, grated
- 3/4 cup of cheddar cheese, reduced fat, grated

Directions:

1. Preheat the Air fryer to 356 degrees.
2. Spread butter on a slice of bread. Place inside the cooking basket with the butter side facing down.
3. Place cheese and scallions on top. Spread the rest of the butter on the other slice of bread Put it on top of the sandwich and sprinkle with parmesan cheese.
4. Cook for 10 minutes.

Nutrition: Calorie: 154Carbohydrate: 9g Fat: 2.5g Protein: 8.6g Fiber: 2.4g

Lean Lamb and Turkey Meatballs with Yogurt

Preparation Time: 10 minutes

Servings: 4

Cooking Time: 8 minutes

Ingredients:

- 1 egg white
- 4 ounces ground lean turkey
- 1 pound of ground lean lamb
- 1 teaspoon each of cayenne pepper, ground coriander, red chili pastes, salt, and ground cumin
- 2 garlic cloves, minced
- 1 1/2 tablespoons parsley, chopped
- 1 tablespoon mint, chopped
- 1/4 cup of olive oil

For the yogurt

- 2 tablespoons of buttermilk
- 1 garlic clove, minced
- 1/4 cup mint, chopped
- 1/2 cup of Greek yogurt, non-fat
- Salt to taste

Directions:

1. Set the Air Fryer to 390 degrees.
2. Mix all the ingredients for the meatballs in a bowl. Roll and mold them into golf-size round pieces. Arrange in the cooking basket. Cook for 8 minutes.
3. While waiting, combine all the ingredients for the mint yogurt in a bowl. Mix well.

4. Serve the meatballs with the mint yogurt. Top with olives and fresh mint.

5. Nutrition: Calorie: 154 Carbohydrate: 9g Fat: 2.5g Protein: 8.6g Fiber: 2.4g

Air Fried Section and Tomato

Preparation Time: 10 minutes
Cooking Time: 5 minutes
Servings: 2
Ingredients:

- 1 aubergine, sliced thickly into 4 disks

- 1 tomato, sliced into 2 thick disks

- 2 tsp. feta cheese, reduced fat

- 2 fresh basil leaves, minced

- 2 balls, small buffalo mozzarella, reduced fat, roughly torn

- Pinch of salt

- Pinch of black pepper

Directions:

1. Preheat Air Fryer to 330 degrees F.

2. Spray small amount of oil into the Air fryer basket. Fry aubergine slices for 5 minutes or until golden brown on both sides. Transfer to a plate.

3. Fry tomato slices in batches for 5 minutes or until seared on both sides.

4. To serve, stack salad starting with an aborigine base, buffalo mozzarella, basil leaves, tomato slice, and 1/2-teaspoon feta cheese.

5. Top of with another slice of aborigine and 1/2 tsp. feta cheese. Serve.

Nutrition: Calorie: 140.3Carbohydrate: 26.6Fat: 3.4g Protein: 4.2g Fiber: 7.3g

Cheesy Salmon Fillets

Preparation Time: 15 minutes

Cooking Time: 20 minutes

Servings: 2-3

Ingredients: For the salmon fillets

- 2 pieces, 4 oz. each salmon fillets, choose even cuts

- 1/2 cup sour cream, reduced fat

- ¼ cup cottage cheese, reduced fat

- ¼ cup Parmigiano-Reggiano cheese, freshly grated

Garnish:

- Spanish paprika

- 1/2 piece lemon, cut into wedges

Directions:

1. Preheat Air Fryer to 330 degrees F.

2. To make the salmon fillets, mix sour cream, cottage cheese, and Parmigiano-Reggiano cheese in a bowl.

3. Layer salmon fillets in the Air fryer basket. Fry for 20 minutes or until cheese turns golden brown.

4. To assemble, place a salmon fillet and sprinkle paprika. Garnish with lemon wedges and squeeze lemon juice on top. Serve.

Nutrition: Calorie: 274Carbohydrate: 1g Fat: 19g Protein: 24g Fiber: 0.5g

Salmon with Asparagus

Preparation Time: 5 Minutes

Cooking Time: 10 Minutes

Servings: 3

Ingredients:

- 1 lb. Salmon, sliced into fillets
- 1 tbsp. Olive Oil
- Salt & Pepper, as needed
- 1 bunch of Asparagus, trimmed
- 2 cloves of Garlic, minced
- Zest & Juice of 1/2 Lemon
- 1 tbsp. Butter, salted

Directions:

1. Spoon in the butter and olive oil into a large pan and heat it over medium-high heat.
2. Once it becomes hot, place the salmon and season it with salt and pepper.
3. Cook for 4 minutes per side and then cook the other side.
4. Stir in the garlic and lemon zest to it.
5. Cook for further 2 minutes or until slightly browned.
6. Off the heat and squeeze the lemon juice over it.
7. Serve it hot.

Nutrition:

Calories: 409Kcal

Carbohydrates: 2.7g

Proteins: 32.8g

Fat: 28.8g

Sodium: 497mg

Shrimp in Garlic Butter

Preparation Time: 5 Minutes
Cooking Time: 20 Minutes
Servings: 4
Ingredients:

- 1 lb. Shrimp, peeled & deveined
- ¼ tsp. Red Pepper Flakes
- 6 tbsp. Butter, divided
- 1/2 cup Chicken Stock
- Salt & Pepper, as needed
- 2 tbsp. Parsley, minced
- 5 cloves of Garlic, minced
- 2 tbsp. Lemon Juice

Directions:

1. Heat a large bottomed skillet over medium-high heat.
2. Spoon in two tablespoons of the butter and melt it. Add the shrimp.
3. Season it with salt and pepper. Sear for 4 minutes or until shrimp gets cooked.
4. Transfer the shrimp to a plate and stir in the garlic.
5. Sauté for 30 seconds or until aromatic.
6. Pour the chicken stock and whisk it well. Allow it to simmer for 5 to 10 minutes or until it has reduced to half.
7. Spoon the remaining butter, red pepper, and lemon juice to the sauce. Mix.
8. Continue cooking for another 2 minutes.
9. Take off the pan from the heat and add the cooked shrimp to it.

10. Garnish with parsley and transfer to the serving bowl.

11. Enjoy.

Nutrition:
Calories: 307Kcal
Carbohydrates: 3g
Proteins: 27g
Fat: 20g
Sodium: 522mg

Cobb Salad

Keto & Under 30 Minutes

Preparation Time: 5 Minutes
Cooking Time: 5 Minutes
Servings: 1
Ingredients:
- 4 Cherry Tomatoes, chopped
- ¼ cup Bacon, cooked & crumbled
- 1/2 of 1 Avocado, chopped
- 2 oz. Chicken Breast, shredded
- 1 Egg, hardboiled
- 2 cups Mixed Green salad
- 1 oz. Feta Cheese, crumbled

Directions:
1. Toss all the ingredients for the Cobb salad in a large mixing bowl and toss well.
2. Serve and enjoy it.

Nutrition:
Calories: 307Kcal
Carbohydrates: 3g
Proteins: 27g
Fat: 20g
Sodium: 522mg

Seared Tuna Steak

Preparation Time: 10 Minutes
Cooking Time: 10 Minutes
Serving Size: 2
Ingredients:

- 1 tsp. Sesame Seeds
- 1 tbsp. Sesame Oil
- 2 tbsp. Soya Sauce
- Salt & Pepper, to taste
- 2 × 6 oz. Ahi Tuna Steaks

Directions:

1. Seasoning the tuna steaks with salt and pepper. Keep it aside on a shallow bowl.
2. In another bowl, mix soya sauce and sesame oil.
3. pour the sauce over the salmon and coat them generously with the sauce.
4. Keep it aside for 10 to 15 minutes and then heat a large skillet over medium heat.
5. Once hot, keep the tuna steaks and cook them for 3 minutes or until seared underneath.
6. Flip the fillets and cook them for a further 3 minutes.
7. Transfer the seared tuna steaks to the serving plate and slice them into 1/2 inch slices. Top with sesame seeds.

Nutrition:

Calories: 255Kcal

Fat: 9g

Carbohydrates: 1g

Proteins: 40.5g

Sodium: 293mg

Beef Chili

Preparation Time: 10 Minutes
Cooking Time: 20 Minutes
Serving Size: 4
Ingredients:

- 1/2 tsp. Garlic Powder
- 1 tsp. Coriander, grounded
- 1 lb. Beef, grounded
- 1/2 tsp. Sea Salt
- 1/2 tsp. Cayenne Pepper
- 1 tsp. Cumin, grounded
- 1/2 tsp. Pepper, grounded
- 1/2 cup Salsa, low-carb & no-sugar

Directions:

1. Heat a large-sized pan over medium-high heat and cook the beef in it until browned.
2. Stir in all the spices and cook them for 7 minutes or until everything is combined.
3. When the beef gets cooked, spoon in the salsa.
4. Bring the mixture to a simmer and cook for another 8 minutes or until everything comes together.
5. Take it from heat and transfer to a serving bowl.

Nutrition:
Calories: 229Kcal
Fat: 10g
Carbohydrates: 2g
Proteins: 33g
Sodium: 675mg

Greek Broccoli Salad

Preparation Time: 10 Minutes
Cooking Time: 15 Minutes
Servings: 4
Ingredients:

- 1 ¼ lb. Broccoli, sliced into small bites
- ¼ cup Almonds, sliced
- 1/3 cup Sun-dried Tomatoes
- ¼ cup Feta Cheese, crumbled
- ¼ cup Red Onion, sliced

For the dressing:

- 1/4 cup Olive Oil
- Dash of Red Pepper Flakes
- 1 Garlic clove, minced
- ¼ tsp. Salt
- 2 tbsp. Lemon Juice
- 1/2 tsp. Dijon Mustard
- 1 tsp. Low Carb Sweetener Syrup
- 1/2 tsp. Oregano, dried

Directions:

1. Mix broccoli, onion, almonds and sun-dried tomatoes in a large mixing bowl.
2. In another small-sized bowl, combine all the dressing ingredients until emulsified.
3. Spoon the dressing over the broccoli salad.
4. Allow the salad to rest for half an hour before serving.

Nutrition:
Calories: 272Kcal
Carbohydrates: 11.9g
Proteins: 8g
Fat: 21.6g
Sodium: 321mg

Cheesy Cauliflower Gratin

Preparation Time: 5 Minutes

Cooking Time: 25 Minutes

Servings: 6

Ingredients:

- 6 deli slices Pepper Jack Cheese
- 4 cups Cauliflower florets
- Salt and Pepper, as needed
- 4 tbsp. Butter
- 1/3 cup Heavy Whipping Cream

Directions:

1. Mix the cauliflower, cream, butter, salt, and pepper in a safe microwave bowl and combine well.
2. Microwave the cauliflower mixture for 25 minutes on high until it becomes soft and tender.
3. Remove the ingredients from the bowl and mash with the help of a fork.
4. Taste for seasonings and spoon in salt and pepper as required.
5. Arrange the slices of pepper jack cheese on top of the cauliflower mixture and microwave for 3 minutes until the cheese starts melting.
6. Serve warm.

Nutrition:

Calories: 421Kcal

Carbohydrates: 3g

Proteins: 19g

Fat: 37g

Sodium: 111mg

Strawberry Spinach Salad

Preparation Time: 5 Minutes

Cooking Time: 10 Minutes

Servings: 4

Ingredients:

- 4 oz. Feta Cheese, crumbled
- 8 Strawberries, sliced
- 2 oz. Almonds
- 6 Slices Bacon, thick-cut, crispy and crumbled
- 10 oz. Spinach leaves, fresh
- 2 Roma Tomatoes, diced
- 2 oz. Red Onion, sliced thinly

Directions:

1. For making this healthy salad, mix all the ingredients needed to make the salad in a large-sized bowl and toss them well.

Nutrition:

Calories – 255kcal

Fat – 16g

Carbohydrates – 8g

Proteins – 14g

Sodium: 27mg

Cauliflower Mac & Cheese

Preparation Time: 5 Minutes

Cooking Time: 25 Minutes

Effort: Easy

Serving Size: 4

Ingredients:

- 1 Cauliflower Head, torn into florets
- Salt & Black Pepper, as needed
- ¼ cup Almond Milk, unsweetened
- ¼ cup Heavy Cream
- 3 tbsp. Butter, preferably grass-fed
- 1 cup Cheddar Cheese, shredded

Directions:

1. Preheat the oven to 450 F.
2. Melt the butter in a small microwave-safe bowl and heat it for 30 seconds.
3. Pour the melted butter over the cauliflower florets along with salt and pepper. Toss them well.
4. Place the cauliflower florets in a parchment paper-covered large baking sheet.
5. Bake them for 15 minutes or until the cauliflower is crisp-tender.
6. Once baked, mix the heavy cream, cheddar cheese, almond milk, and the remaining butter in a large microwave-safe bowl and heat it on high heat for 2 minutes or until the cheese mixture is smooth. Repeat the procedure until the cheese has melted.
7. Finally, stir in the cauliflower to the sauce mixture and coat well.

Nutrition:
Calories: 294Kcal
Fat: 23g
Carbohydrates: 7g
Proteins: 11g

Easy Egg Salad

Preparation Time: 5 Minutes

Cooking Time: 15 to 20 Minutes

Effort: Easy

Servings: 4

Ingredients:

- 6 Eggs, preferably free-range
- ¼ tsp. Salt
- 2 tbsp. Mayonnaise
- 1 tsp. Lemon juice
- 1 tsp. Dijon mustard
- Pepper, to taste
- Lettuce leaves, to serve

Directions:

1. Keep the eggs in a saucepan of water and pour cold water until it covers the egg by another 1 inch.
2. Bring to a boil and then remove the eggs from heat.
3. Peel the eggs under cold running water.
4. Transfer the cooked eggs into a food processor and pulse them until chopped.
5. Stir in the mayonnaise, lemon juice, salt, Dijon mustard, and pepper and mix them well.
6. Taste for seasoning and add more if required.
7. Serve in the lettuce leaves.

Nutrition:

Calories – 166kcal

Fat – 14g

Carbohydrates - 0.85g

Proteins – 10g

Sodium: 132mg

Baked Chicken Legs

Preparation Time: 10 Minutes
Cooking Time: 40 Minutes
Effort: Easy
Servings: 6
Ingredients:

- 6 Chicken Legs
- ¼ tsp. Black Pepper
- ¼ cup Butter
- 1/2 tsp. Sea Salt
- 1/2 tsp. Smoked Paprika
- 1/2 tsp. Garlic Powder

Directions:

1. Preheat the oven to 425 F.

2. Pat the chicken legs with a paper towel to absorb any excess moisture.

3. Marinate the chicken pieces by first applying the butter over them and then with the seasoning. Set it aside for a few minutes.

4. Bake them for 25 minutes. Turnover and bake for further 10 minutes or until the internal temperature reaches 165 F.

5. Serve them hot.

Nutrition:
Calories – 236kL
Fat – 16g
Carbohydrates – 0g
Protein – 22g
Sodium – 314mg

Creamed Spinach

Preparation Time: 5 Minutes
Cooking Time: 10 Minutes
Effort: Easy
Servings: 4
Ingredients:

- 3 tbsp. Butter
- ¼ tsp. Black Pepper
- 4 cloves of Garlic, minced
- ¼ tsp. Sea Salt
- 10 oz. Baby Spinach, chopped
- 1 tsp. Italian Seasoning
- 1/2 cup Heavy Cream
- 3 oz. Cream Cheese

Directions:

1. Melt butter in a large sauté pan over medium heat.

2. Once the butter has melted, spoon in the garlic and sauté for 3o seconds or until aromatic.

3. Spoon in the spinach and cook for 3 to 4 minutes or until wilted.

4. Add all the remaining ingredients to it and continuously stir until the cream cheese melts and the mixture gets thickened.

5. Serve hot

Nutrition:
Calories – 274kL
Fat – 27g

Carbohydrates – 4g
Protein – 4g
Sodium – 114mg

Stuffed Mushrooms

Preparation Time: 10 Minutes
Cooking Time: 20 Minutes
Servings: 4
Ingredients:
- 4 Portobello Mushrooms, large
- 1/2 cup Mozzarella Cheese, shredded
- 1/2 cup Marinara, low-sugar
- Olive Oil Spray

Directions:
1. Preheat the oven to 375 F.

2. Take out the dark gills from the mushrooms with the help of a spoon.

3. Keep the mushroom stem upside down and spoon it with two tablespoons of marinara sauce and mozzarella cheese.

4. Bake for 18 minutes or until the cheese is bubbly.

Nutrition:
Calories – 113kL
Fat – 6g
Carbohydrates – 4g
Protein – 7g
Sodium – 14mg

Vegetable Soup

Preparation Time: 10 Minutes
Cooking Time: 30 Minutes
Servings: 5
Ingredients:

- 8 cups Vegetable Broth
- 2 tbsp. Olive Oil
- 1 tbsp. Italian Seasoning
- 1 Onion, large & diced
- 2 Bay Leaves, dried
- 2 Bell Pepper, large & diced
- Sea Salt & Black Pepper, as needed
- 4 cloves of Garlic, minced
- 28 oz. Tomatoes, diced
- 1 Cauliflower head, medium & torn into florets
- 2 cups Green Beans, trimmed & chopped

Directions:

1. Heat oil in a Dutch oven over medium heat.

2. Once the oil becomes hot, stir in the onions and pepper.

3. Cook for 10 minutes or until the onion is softened and browned.

4. Spoon in the garlic and sauté for a minute or until fragrant.

5. Add all the remaining ingredients to it. Mix until everything comes together.

6. Bring the mixture to a boil. Lower the heat and cook for further 20 minutes or until the vegetables have softened.

7. Serve hot.

Nutrition:
Calories – 79kL
Fat – 2g
Carbohydrates – 8g
Protein – 2g
Sodium – 187mg

Pork Chop Diane

Preparation Time: 10 minutes
Cooking Time: 20 minutes
Serving: 4
Ingredients:

- ¼ cup low-sodium chicken broth

- 1 tablespoon freshly squeezed lemon juice

- 2 teaspoons Worcestershire sauce

- 2 teaspoons Dijon mustard

- 4 (5-ounce) boneless pork top loin chops

- 1 teaspoon extra-virgin olive oil

- 1 teaspoon lemon zest

- 1 teaspoon butter

- 2 teaspoons chopped fresh chives

Direction:

1. Blend together the chicken broth, lemon juice, Worcestershire sauce, and Dijon mustard and set it aside.

2. Season the pork chops lightly.

3. Situate large skillet over medium-high heat and add the olive oil.

4. Cook the pork chops, turning once, until they are no longer pink, about 8 minutes per side.

5. Put aside the chops.

6. Pour the broth mixture into the skillet and cook until warmed through and thickened, about 2 minutes.

7. Blend lemon zest, butter, and chives.

8. Garnish with a generous spoonful of sauce.

Nutrition:
200 Calories
8g Fat
1g Carbohydrates

Autumn Pork Chops with Red Cabbage and Apples

Preparation Time: 15 minutes
Cooking Time: 30 minutes
Serving: 4
Ingredients:

- ¼ cup apple cider vinegar

- 2 tablespoons granulated sweetener

- 4 (4-ounce) pork chops, about 1 inch thick

- 1 tablespoon extra-virgin olive oil

- ½ red cabbage, finely shredded

- 1 sweet onion, thinly sliced

- 1 apple, peeled, cored, and sliced

- 1 teaspoon chopped fresh thyme

Direction:

1. Scourge together the vinegar and sweetener. Set it aside.

2. Season the pork with salt and pepper.

3. Position huge skillet over medium-high heat and add the olive oil.

4. Cook the pork chops until no longer pink, turning once, about 8 minutes per side.

5. Put chops aside.

6. Add the cabbage and onion to the skillet and sauté until the vegetables have softened, about 5 minutes.

7. Add the vinegar mixture and the apple slices to the skillet and bring the mixture to a boil.

8. Adjust heat to low and simmer, covered, for 5 additional minutes.

9. Return the pork chops to the skillet, along with any accumulated juices and thyme, cover, and cook for 5 more minutes.

Nutrition:
223 Calories
12g Carbohydrates
3g Fiber

New years day
is black

*The publisher wishes to thank InterAnima CIC
and Becalelis Brodskis*

Dolf Mootham, Eimear McBride and Ray Rumsby

UNESCO *City of Literature* ™

First published in 2016

by Propolis Books
The Book Hive
53 London Street
Norwich NR2 1HL

www.propolisbooks.co.uk

design by Niki Medlik at **studio medlikova**

A CIP record for this book
is available from the British Library

Printed and Bound in the UK by the Pureprint Group

Nicky Loutit

with an introduction by D. J. Taylor

New years day is black

An artist's journey
through memory

Nicky Loutit.

propolis

Dedicated to 'The Freshes'

INTRODUCTION
by D. J. Taylor

For a direct route into the world where Nicky Loutit spent her formative years, you need only turn to the mid-1940s correspondence of Evelyn Waugh. Here is the author of the newly-published *Brideshead Revisited* in August 1945 offering Patrick Balfour a gossipy update on the doings of their mutual friend Cyril Connolly: 'He and Mrs Lubbock have imposed on a dead-end kid named Jacqueline, a former connection of yours, half-sister of Angela; she has bare feet like a camel…and a baby by a communist doctor.' The dead-end kid, whose name Waugh lazily mishears, now found sharing a house in Regent's Park with Connolly and his long-term girlfriend Lys, is Nicky's mother Janetta. The baby is Nicky herself. There is further mention of Janetta in a letter of April 1948 to Nancy Mitford, which brings tidings of 'a new look: silk stockings, high-heeled shoes, diamond clips everywhere' (a description which Nicky finds impossible to imagine), and a passing reference to her in Waugh's last novel *Unconditional Surrender* (1961), where she appears as one of the 'veiled ladies'- the attentive secretaries who assist 'Everard Spruce' (a lightly disguised portrait of Connolly) in producing his war-time magazine *Survival* (an even less lightly-disguised portrait of Connolly's *Horizon*). The secretaries are said to be dressed rather like their employer 'though in commoner materials: they wore their hair long and enveloping, in a style which fifteen years later was to be associated by the newspapers with the King's Road. One went bare-footed as though to emphasize her servile condition.' That this is a mischievous portrait of Janetta seems evident from the fact that, when briefly employed by Connolly in the early 1940s and prone to wander shoeless around the office, she was nicknamed 'Miss Bluefeet' by the *Horizon* cognoscenti. And already, as the literary landscapes of the late

1940s wheel once more into view and Waugh, Connolly and Nancy Mitford spring up to populate them, the paralysing interpretative danger posed by a book like *New Year's Day Is Black* will have begun to declare itself: the temptation to focus on its milieu and the famous names who march around in it, rather than to concentrate on the personality of its author - a woman who, almost from the moment of her birth, was relegated to its margin and seems to have spent most of the rest of her life trying to come to terms with her exclusion.

As she admits to being 'terrible about dates', a few biographical details may be necessary. Nicolette ('Nicky') Loutit was born on 11 June 1943, the daughter and first child of Janetta Slater (*nee* Woolley, b.1922) and Kenneth Sinclair-Loutit (1913-2003), whose name her mother adopted by deed poll. Janetta had already pursued an adventurous career, escaping from Spain in a British destroyer after the Nationalist attack on Malaga and marrying the writer and Civil War veteran Humphrey Slater before she was out of her teens. Sinclair-Loutit, too, was an old Spanish hand, a Cambridge graduate who had temporarily abandoned his medical studies to enlist in the Marxist International Brigade and incurred the lasting enmity of the Trotskyist militia-supporting George Orwell. According to a tantalising fragment from Sinclair-Loutit's unpublished autobiography, *Very Little Luggage*, the two of them met in a Barcelona café in May 1937 to discuss the progress of the war. Orwell, suspicious of his comrade's political sympathies, kept his cards close to his chest.

'Intellectual and left-wing' as Nicky puts it, Janetta's circle was also resolutely bohemian. It included Connolly – at this point in an erratic career perhaps the most influential literary critic in England – the second generation Bloomsbury-ites Frances and Ralph Partridge and, by way of her friendship with Sonia Brownell, another of the *Horizon* sorority, art-world types like the young painters Lucian Freud and Michael Wishart. Through Sonia, soon to become the second Mrs Orwell, she knew the author of *Nineteen Eighty-Four*, whose hospital bed Nicky remembers visiting shortly before his death in January 1950. There was even an unrealised plan that mother and daughter could pay an extended visit to Orwell's hideaway on the island of Jura where Nicky, as well as enjoying the Hebridean air, might prove herself a suitable same-age companion for Orwell's adopted son Richard. 'I wrote to Genetta [*sic* – what *was* it about Janetta's name that no senior literary man seems able to reproduce it?]' Orwell informed Sonia in April 1947, 'asking her to come whenever she liked & giving instructions about the journey. So long as she's bringing the child and not just sending it, it should be simple enough.'

In the event, Janetta cried off: there were other fish to fry. By this time she had drifted apart from Sinclair-Loutit and taken up with the writer and broadcaster Robert Kee, living with him either in the house at Regent's Park whose middle-floor, sandwiched between their living space and bedrooms, was tenanted by Connolly, or as guests of the Partridges at Ham Spray on the Hampshire-Wiltshire border. The couple were married in January 1948, but by early 1950 the relationship was in trouble. In the summer of 1950 Janetta departed for the south of France with Derek Jackson, an immensely wealthy and fascist-sympathising professor of Spectroscopy, then married to Pamela Mitford. Jackson and Janetta married in 1951.

Nicky, meanwhile, was enduring a peripatetic childhood, in which occasional moments of serenity alternated with bewildering interludes of exile and abandonment. A certain amount of time was spent in a children's home, still more in a succession of boarding schools. Home life, when it existed, was subject to endless stress and fracture: 'Nicky reacts in her own way to the situation' runs a worried entry from Frances Partridge's diary in November 1945, 'and at breakfast she entered the room at a red-faced tearful gallop, one arm outstretched towards Janetta, a tiny Tintoretto bacchante.' Of her step-fathers, she remembers Robert Kee as a man who shouted at her, and in addition 'wanted to kill her.' Jackson, less flagrantly hostile, had his own methods of making his step-daughter feel small. These included setting her tests in mathematics and spelling and showing no sympathy whatever when she failed to shape up, and visiting her at Frensham Heights, the expensive boarding establishment whose fees he paid and steering her round and round the rose beds in his Buick, not caring about the embarrassment he caused. Her impression, as his biographer Simon Courtauld puts it, 'was that he wanted her to feel stupid; she was in the way…' Meeting her several years later at a lunch party in Paris, (by this time Derek had abandoned Janetta for the half-sister mentioned in Evelyn Waugh's letter), he enquired if she remembered 'all the nice times we had together.' 'No' Nicky assured him.

If there was a respite from these years of being passed around the Home Counties like a piece of superfluous baggage, it came in the regular visits to Ham Spray. The Partridges' brand of well-heeled high-mindedness has come in for a fair amount of mockery since its exposure in Frances' various volumes of diaries – see, in particular, V.S. Pritchett's story *Cocky Olly* – but Frances and Ralph liked and sympathised with Nicky, were kind to her and offered a bolt-hole to which she constantly returned until her eventual departure to the first of two prestigious London art schools in the early Sixties. 'Back they all came' Frances writes in January 1951, of the sudden descent of mother, daughter and Georgiana, Janetta's child by Robert Kee, 'Nicky – poor little creature – intoxicated by her school clothes and the vista of life that they invoke. What pleases her most is her school tie – a horrid shiny green-striped one – and she insisted on putting it on at once.' Haunted by the ghosts of Bloomsbury – Lytton, Carrington and Virginia – Ham Spray acted as a magnet for survivors from this vanished age. These included the elderly Saxon Sydney-Turner, who fascinated the small girl with what Frances calls 'his almost invisible nods and gestures.'

As the record of a life, *New Year's Day Is Black* is a deeply impressionistic piece of work. Great stretches of the author's life, notably the time spent in India in the 1970s at the mercy of a sinister religious cult, are mentioned only in parenthesis and her 30 year marriage to the writer Jonathan Gathorne-Hardy is omitted altogether. What follows is a story of neglect and abuse - most of it courtesy of her biological father - but also of survival and, in the end, renewal. What remains is a painfully honest attempt to understand the bygone life of which she was a part and its effect on the person she came to be - a stealthy critique of what might be called 'Bloomsbury' attitudes to personal relationships and parenting that ranks alongside Angelica Garnett's *Deceived with Kindness*. It is a quietly devastating book, which deserves the widest possible circulation – whether the reader happens to be interested in Connolly, Orwell, Frances and Ralph Partridge or simply the fate of small children left to their own devices while the noise of the adult world booms on terrifyingly in the endlessly disputed space above their heads.

www.nickyloutit.co.uk
www.propolisbooks.co.uk

New years day is black

Most Days,
Unwilling, but doing it: going for a walk:

One of my favorite places is the
Freshes ~ where river water meets the
Sea.

in the winter

And floating with the tide in the summer

This morning I met a Lady of 81
— ten years older than me.

We began to talk

OH I LIKE COFFE

YES YES SO DO I

Once I get back home

YES

I'm always doing that

How many sons do you have ??

I do 3 miles most days
me too
I text my son once I'm out here
Do you use ready made meals?
me too, yes & send them photos
yes Waitrose macaroni cheese
I'll just sit here for a while

So everything is fine
Just ordinarily fine

But back home . . . . .

ALL MY PAINTINGS

ALL THOSE OPPORTUNITIES
THAT WORK
NO
ONE SEES IT
An unharnessed talent . . . . .

I went to Chelsea Art School, where
Lawrence Gowing was in charge, and he
employed painters he admired who mostly
worked with us in the Life studios. I was
impressed and inspired by so many of
them, and then I went to the Slade and
again I met so much to help me, though
I was lonely and an outsider, longing
not to be, I had a love affair with my
tutor, we talked painting I was in and out
of his paintings, I was so stirred I spent
too much time crying, or being an old
fashioned artist in Soho. I smoked woodbines,
wore a duffel jacket, and spent much passion
in drawing in Leon Kossoffs evening class.
No lights - our drawings dissapeared as
night darkness matched our dark attempts.

Is it possible I've done it? I've done good paintings and bad ones. Have I finished? And who was that lady anyway, sitting on a tump like a Giotto angel?

I wonder as I breathe out

My work scattering behind me

I wonder again as I breathe out — my ribs are too big —

my father a DOCTER said so

Though he was a Monster I believed him...

I Don't Know where I Stand

OR HOW TO

Falling down OH NO NO I'M-DOWN

Before I die I want to be foursquare
And I still haven't found my feet.

Nor my face

Who's that? That's YOU

You

To be foursquare I must stop thinking
I'm ugly, nearly the last hurdle.

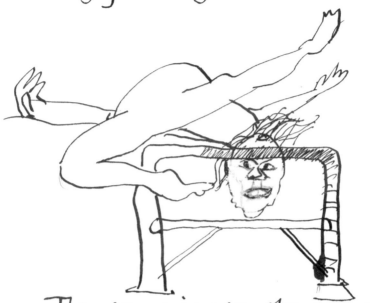

The fence is very strong and high.

As a child I was
told that I must
keep my nose
clean as people
could see so
easily up it

TODAY, I'm at a loss

I AM
HERE

[I'm right handed
But copying myself
comes out
like this]

Some day
in late April
2015

An insignificant failure

A creative dreamer
unsurpassed beauty flows beyond

A few weeks ago my very old mother said in a hopeless tone of voice, talking about my father

I simply couldn't bear to touch him - too awful

I couldn't help it

And, I don't remember my mother touching me.

My body was very flexible

My skin had a yellowish tinge

My father demonstrated my huge wrist bones

As the War ended my father dissapeared, and my 1st Stepfather appeared. He was handsome and charming and angry. My mother loved him, though he wanted to kill me. He had been a prisoner of war, a pilot, shot down over the iced up sea.

ROBERT

I drove him mad, or mader still.

JUST SHUT UP SHUT UP SHUT UP

OH GOD

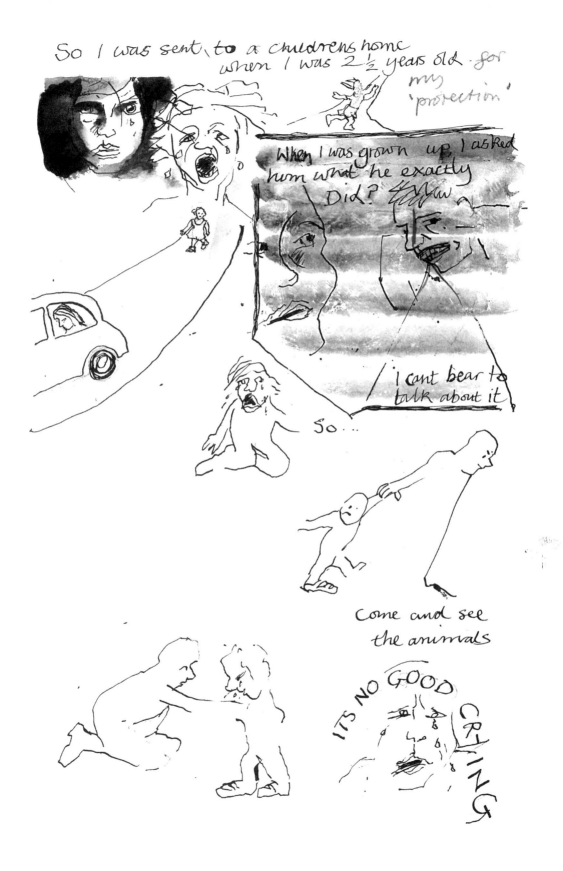

So I was sent to a childrens home
when I was 2½ years old for
my
'protection'

When I was grown up, I asked
him what he exactly
Did?

I cant bear to
talk about it

So...

Come and see
the animals

ITS NO GOOD CRYING

—— Now stop Crying ——

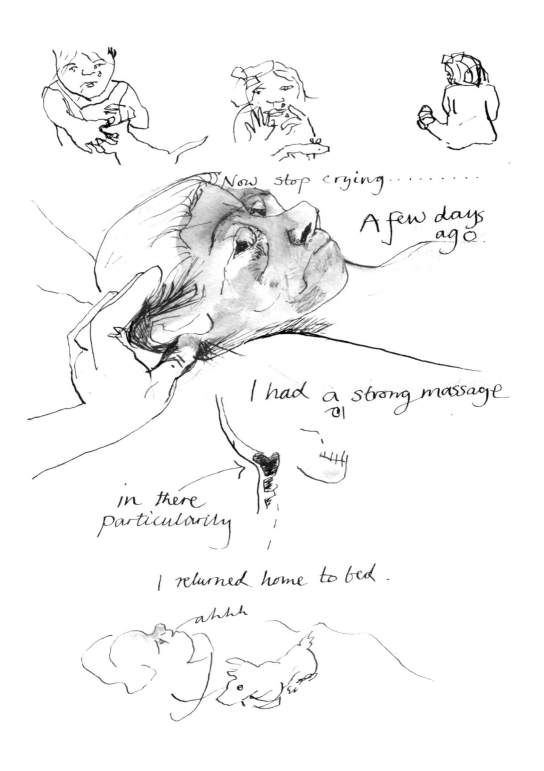

I took the most terrible risk and floated calmly up out of the deep sea. The dream gives me goose pimples

But

Although the jump was scarey and I upset the people I was with, the calm, rising up to the air was wonderful despite the terrible memory that came with it.

Its all in that photo Album.

All of us squashed in

I HATE THAT ALBUM OR DO I ?

40 years ago We were living on our small holding ,me, my husband Patrick , Becalelis, my first son from a previous marriage ,and Noa , and baby Joseph . we were Happy , hard working,idealistic following the wave of self sufficiency that was going on then , and ,unfortunately seeking a religion . We thought we had found the answer with 'Rajneesh '. Terrible to even write his name , but then he was our god . We were going to go and live with the community in Poona .

WITH LOVE AND HIS BLESSINGS ~

We had to "give up everything" and give it to him

" This moment contains all that is possible and all that is impossible too everything converges on this moment"

room where Joseph was Borne

TODAY

TODAY

TODAY

How ? Why ? What ?

And the 'freshes walk again to sort things OUT

MAKES NO Difference which way I jump

Best put it out then... like the dream rise up!

Odd to have a releasing dream 30 years later - could be I'm ahead of myself.

Can I say I was brainwashed?

YOU'RE FULL OF ANGER

go into the flow

your love is possesive

HEY COME ON!

Oh wow you will really blossom we just love our master it's just so beautiful

Come and be part of the family

it's all ego - just ego. Just let gooow

give the kids to the cosmos

To India

I put my eldest son Becalelis in a terrible
posiotion. His father, a French Moroccan
jew didn't want Becalelis to come with
us. I was torn, and asked Rajneesh
what I should do. The reply was let the
child choose - Kids are the wise ones.

My master SAYS

Our beloved Master Says

NO
NO
NEVER
EVER

I'LL NEVER
Let him
go
There

Becatelis
'chose'

I Let him
go with his
father

It's hard to wash deeds away. There's
something about the plainess of Norfolk
that helps. Plain miraculous.

years of washing
washing
away
washing through

Sitting on the salt marsh, with my sketch Book.

honk honk

COLD HANDS

Early morning, low tide, golden water seeps through the mud. I can hear it, collecting as the sea pushes inland.

Blue!

the sea

all the way from the sea

Blue

and back again

The marvelous, miraculous pieces of my life was the birth of my 3 Sons. Giving birth was something I could do. It was a powerful experience. Each birth different, and so they remain, but continue to be central to me.

I've asked them to contribute their memories of the ghastly Rajneesh days, as in washing out my own I wonder how its left them.

PUSH
PUSH
PUSH

IAM

The 1st giving birth
in Hospital then

MY GRATUDE TO SHIELA KITZINGER A 'PSYCHSEXUAL

BECALELIS

NOA

JOSEPH

'Aproach'

Becalelis' Contribution

The black eyes I got in a group - a 'therapy' group called ENCOUNTER. It was for those Rajneesh considered needed a particularly strong push. Those (wise ones I now see) who wouldn't 'let go'. It was known as the no limitations group. It was my award/punishment for freaking out early one morning during the very demanding work in the busy kitchen. I immersed myself in that group - 7 days and nights in a padded underground room - desperate to find out how to be happy in the Ashram. I got 1 black eye from a punch, and the 2nd diving off a human pyramid onto the floor. I learnt how hellish hell is.

Now I feel a terrible sadness that any of us went through that.

I left some money - with Becalelis' Father - to pay for him to come and visit us in Poona.

Noa's part

WE GOT OFF THE LONG FLIGHT

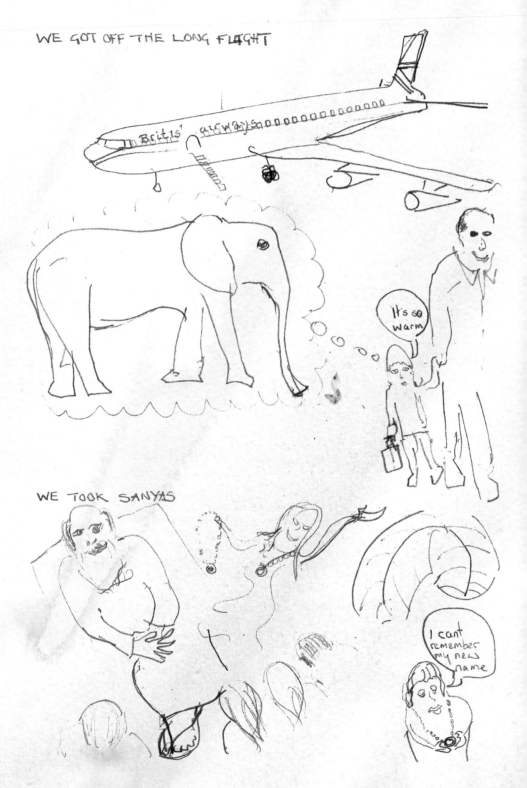

WE TOOK SANYAS

I LISTENED TO THE MAN
SWEEPING

MY BROTHER WAS SWITCHED WITH ANOTHER BABY, FOR
BREASTFEEDING.   EVERYONE LAUGHED.

Josephs contribution

I was too young to remember anything except a long table with a pot of honey and a pig snuffling to eat my poo in the street. I'm not even sure I remember that. My dad tells me it was a journey into the light.

(5 years old)

Mu My mum tells me it was a terrible dark tunnel.

Whatever it was it changed my life.

This is 'Osho'. Not my dad, or a hipster.

I'm not very good at drawing.

?

In fact I probably only wrote 'whatever' out of loyalty to my dad. That man Osho has scary eyes.

I'd allocated a different colour
to each son, and wanted the colours
as a background to their words. I didn't
tell them, it wasn't important enough.

I was pleased — interested when Joseph
chose to do his bit on a pale blue
background — the colour he was born
into — the colour I painted our bedroom
in Herefordshire, knowing I'd give
birth there, & the colour I'd
allocated for him.

Certainly whatever was going on in my head wasn't in my heart. Much has faded with shame, anger, incredulaty. Our 1st morning in Poona is still vivid though - perhaps because it gives me a nugget of understanding.

Having sold everything, left our home and donated all to Rajneesh, we arrived in poona exhausted from our journey - a many tiered exhaustion. My husband (since divorced) and our two sons slept on mattreses in an airless hotel room that opened up onto a beautiful garden. I sat near them in my hideous orange robe and cried and cried - yes as in my early childhood. I'd left my eldest son, aged 9 behind, and every scrap of my life - except the 3 people with me - I'd thrown out. I was in this 'magic mystery school'. As I sobbed my new 'friends' gathered round and told me this was my 'blossming', my 'letting go'. I was soon to be flowing with a new understanding & awareness.

I remember the women who told me I was blossoming - I'd known her in London - Her face was soft and sweet, her body lovely, & curved and visibles through her orange robe. I was impressed to see she wasn't wearing knickers. And another London friend was also encouraging

me. They both had a sort of fluidity of
words and movements that I longed to
have too. I cried and cried with a sort
of obedience, believing I might get through
into this new world. I could smell the
earth warming up and see the sky
weighing into its constant heavy blue.
I knew I was in the wrong place but
I felt I'd no alternative. There was only
people to persande me to stay, even
my husband. was convinced we were
doing something utterly wonderful. That
beauty with my two sons stranded in
sleep and heat was Hell. As helpless
as a dumped two year old, I had to
stop crying and be a new woman of 34.

I ESCAPED

LATER 31 YEARS

and NOW NOW NOW

WE LEFT AFTER 5 YEARS

A new life with all 3 sons, and a new husband.
New life into old life, and ageing with
extraordinary people, an expanding
family.

After each memory I have to go on a walk ~ 'walking back to happyness' that song of the 60's, Helen Shapiro ~ Sad to listen to now.

I went through the pine woods, then out to the sea

The trunks below sea level are as roots streatching up into the light. It's as if I'm walking underground, Closer to the underground Angel who lies there.

TODAY AFTER THE DREAM ,AFTER THE ORANGE
MEMORY I FEEL HAPPY IN MY GARDEN .

WHY DOESN'T
MY 'LONDONS PRIDE' .
DO WELL . . . . .

I REMEMBER , THOSE
PLANTS THAT EARTH
THAT SOOT
THOSE HEDGES

After a few months I was out of the
childrens home

Back in
London.
Sussex place
Cyril Connolly and
Lyces?
apartment

MY BED room

my
mother and stepfathers
sitting room and
study

Down there was

my mothers Kitchen

I was obsessed with stairs
Particularly the stair well.

I couldn't read but I lived in book illustrations

MUMFIE

I loved fighting

and snails

and dandy lions

The London house was near the Zoo in Regents Park,
we could hear the distant animal calls
my even more distant father said he would give me
a real baby elephant – from Siam. I planned to
put it where I played in the Laurel bushes.

at night I could
hear it
trumpeting

MY MOTHERS CIRCLE WAS LEFT WING ARTY INTELLECTUAL

We were left on our own to play

Cyril Connolly was the King, even I knew
that, and if he bothered he was nice to me —
despite his quote — one of his many quoted
quotes — 'There is no more Sombre enemy of
good art than the pram in the hall.'
I was aware of important work happening
beneath the social blur of artists, writers
and political minded left wingers.
    Robert Kee was starting his publishing
firm with James MacGibbon.
    I remember my mother drawing a Rose
for the MacGibbon and Key symbol. I was
impressed and felt that the Rose was famous.
    It was Roberts friendship with the MacGibbons
that led me to have 'Little Robert' as my great
friend, and his father James was the kindest
warmest person in my childhood. He'd take
me out from my boarding schools — later —
    I'd stay with his whole family in his house
nearby, and my memory of pure happyness
is riding on his shoulders   and us
both singing "anything   you can
do I can do better"
         "No you can't
          yes you can"

            No you
                    can't"
    "Anything I can do you can't do better"
    -

In our street - Sussex place, there was a large communial garden to share. With 'little Robert' we'de play far away, creeping through the undergrowth near Regents Park canal or balancing for miles - we thought-on garden walls. I'd also play with Tristram Cook - Diana Witherby son - We kept to the garden, with Diana nearby. I was facinated by Diana, but puzzeled that she let her son wear babyish red button shoes.

She had deep brown eyes

that glowed

and

Carefully

put on

Lipstick

She was
a
Poet

and also had a special link with Cyril.

I liked

Sonia Blair / Orwell who was often talking with Diana and my mother. I loved her laugh, it was a rich relief amidst the tense smoking and drinking. I assumed She was really french with her abandon, and dropping french phrases into the talk. She was Kind to me or very impatient - She expected more of me.

Getting old I remember these people more
vividly. Diana Witherby was a part of that chaotic
mix, but slightly seperate. When she was old, and
ill she was wonderfully optomistic, telling me
the advantages of being low down in her wheel
chair, and seeing a different world. I'm only
now reading her poems.

Some moments though struck cleanly into me.
I was aware of much talk about Eric – George
Orwell – between my mother and Sonia

One day my mother was obliged to take me with her to visit Eric. I was happy to be with her, and understood he was ill. (My last memory of him was, him dealing calmly with a broody hen somewhere in the country.)

I was very shocked as we entered his room in the ~~Nursing Home~~ hospital ~ perhaps I'd been told he was dying, but I felt immense fear & care.

I resorted to playing purposefully with my 'dinky' car.

His kindness amazed me — just letting me be.
I didn't see Eric often. I'm told my father and
him argued about their different factions that
they were involved in during the spanish civil
war, but I've few memories of my father, and
I don't remember Eric in sussex place. Though
my mother was with Eric & Sonia when they
got married, at his bedside in the hospital,
a few months before he died.

I was talking to a friend who had a similar upbringing. She said that at least the adults were no longer hidebound, so we learnt a sense of freedom (I was startled to have to credit 'them'). She reminded me too that because the adults were mostly bored by us — to their relief we turned in on ourselves. She was writing plays when she was 11, and 'got the buzz'. I was slower but imagination led me to draw and paint.

One day.—
"From your Father all the way
from Canada"

It could be an elephant...

A special
ski suit
all the
way
from Canada
my *father* sent
it.

ROBERT didn't
like my
suit or
me in
it ...

At the bottom
of the basement
stairs

Quick-back to today.

swimming for old bodies is a release

floating with my granddaughter
in the flow of the tide
is even better.

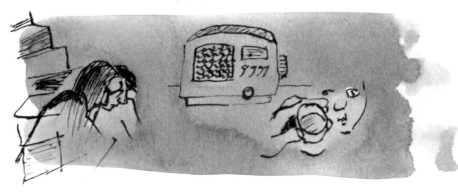

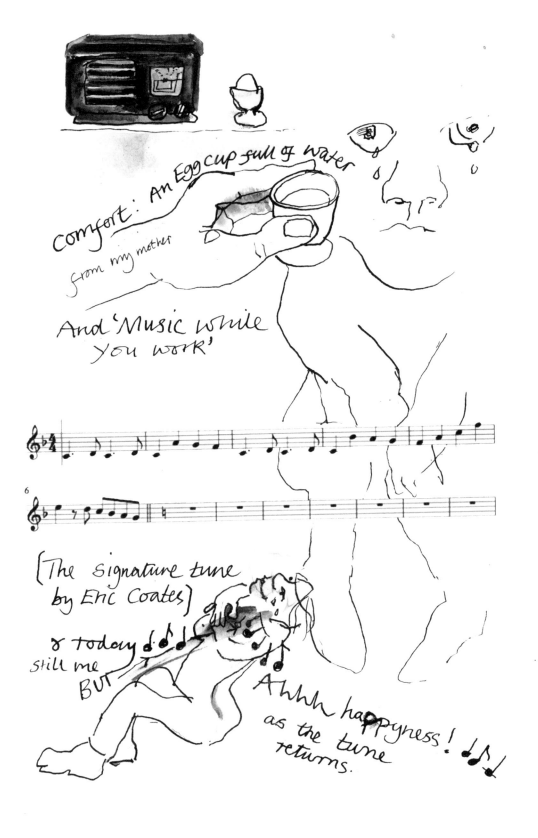

comfort: An Eggcup full of water

from my mother

And 'Music while you work'

[The signature tune by Eric Coates]

& today still me BUT

Ahhh happyness! as the tune returns.

Cyril and his girl friend Lyce, lived in middle floor
I loved to visit
Yes Nicolette, Come in
umm perfume
Can I try Some?
Sure you can
Cyril kept Lemurs.
in his cupboard.

Robert & my mother continued wanting to be rid of me
we frequently went to the country to a house called
Hamspray, where Ralph & Frances & Burgo lived. I used
to think it was called Hamspray because dead pigs
hung in the bathroom to cure for hams. I was also
uneasy about the word 'spray' as I knew somewhere
there had been a violent death — blood stained

Pigs bathroom

'Not in that
room'

Breakfast time

the downs are behind me

It wasn't until I was an adult that I discovered that it was Dora Carrington a painter and Ralph Partridges first wife who had killed herself in that Hamspray bedroom. I only learnt the whole story when jonny my husband was writing his book about Gerald Brenan. For me Ralph & Frances had been together endlessly.

Every morning they'd walk past my bedroom door talking on their way to the end bathroom

And still the name Lyton Strachey, the long thin man that Carrington loved troubles me, as did the portrait of him painted by Carrington. I think there were other long thin drawings of him at Hamspray

Hamspray was the place where terrible rows happened between my mother and stepfather Robert. They chose the lawn to go round and round. I resorted to a hoarding of myself deep within.

...up until 7 it was a place that seeped into me. 64 years later I'm drying out.

Saved by teatime

Walking with memories
of Hanospray.

Tea time

TODAY I ache to use
COLOUR

One last memory of a trick Ralph played.

Interesting that until now I've never mentioned the cat lady - though she's always been here. I invented the cat lady possibley from a real old 'bag lady'. She'd fill her sack with cats, I wasn't sure if she thought she could look after them better, or that she was a frightening thief. She was always polite but insistant and strong. Her nose was hooked, her eyes intense brown, a firm small mouth and olive skin, or was that the smog? She was ageless and powerful.

I once to my mothers annoyance let the cat lady in - my mother said she didn't exsist, but frequently I feared her arrival.

My sister was almost absent in my childhood, and from 7, I was away at boarding schools.
One of the words she uses to describe our childhood is: waiting - we were always waiting

When she was about 3
    She tried to jump on my
    school train ~ about to
depart from Waterloo station.
She was silent and determined
and I was surprised and moved
by her closed little face, pale in the
...rk of Waterloo ~ Waterloo ~
            Waterloo station
[Carved in concrete]
WATERLOO

My mother went to Paris during her divorce
from Robert – to meet my next step father.
Robert was there too, I felt on Roberts side.
At first I stayed in London with the MacGibbons
who I loved, and their youngest son 'Little Robert' was
my good friend, and the same age as me. (he
still has the scar on his arm where I bit
him when I was 2.)

After a few weeks Sonia Orwell took me
to Paris to join the complications. My little
sister was left with Roberts mother. Sonia
gave me a teddy for the 'plane journey.

As I walked happily down the Paris street
with my mother I was proud to be able to
read our hotel sign. LA HOTEL
LOUISIANE   and 66
years
later I
still rember
– only its

LOISIANA
(in my)
heart

It was in Paris that I learnt about colour-
and creating another world as I endlessly
drew and coloured in with thick waxy
crayons that never gave out full flooded
glow. The tones of those colours still
nauseate me ~

              and no longer

ex sist.

The hotel rooms were green
I met my next Stepfather
DEREK.
I'm very rich & very clever
I want you to know that men cry too
and I'm crying Now
YUCK
PARIS CAFE
well done Nicky
I love colouring in
PARIS CAFÉ

Back in London, 1st stepfather gone, 2nd future one - Derek - came to visit. He brought a little boy with him, a replica of himself.

Do you want to come outside & play

We played and played in the garden. Later, I made a cardboard cut out of the boy

and kept him in a cigar box still smelling of cigars.

He had a red tie

a blue jacket

and matching blue trousers

with flaps to bend round his body

My mother moved into Wealth, and &
lived with Derek in Ireland and France.
And I began boarding school that I loved
in many ways. I suppose my new stepfather
Derek payed the bill - not that I was
grateful.

Me proud in uniform

I love my tie

Too awful those clothes

oh well She's very pleased

And I was given a little red 'FAIRY BIKE'

When I was grown up, I discovered that the little identical boy was never there.

I can return him to paper now, but then he was alive, though I had the paper version to keep with me in Cyril's empty cigar box that I treasured. He was called Peter, and was very conventional.

Another walk, back to the place where I met the Old lady. Rain, a rainbow, the skylarks were singing and dipping and lifting above me. Their wings fluttering like butterflys. I worry about their nests on the ground surving. The path was black mud and bright green grass, and I felt strong and Old in my new boots.

I didn't meet anybody. I thought about that Lady....
Has she gone under, dead? or is she still doing her 3 miles a day & texting her Son
OR
Was she an angel a Giotto angel sitting there?
Since then things are changing with my past - fast

Sussex Place, and my mother dims in my memory, but I knew a little about painting. I'd seen my mothers paints laid out and clearly precious to her. I'd been in many other painters studios. I loved looking at paintings, and had gathered that to paint was approved of, and that my interest in it was one good thing about me...

I was 7, I was at Boarding school and I was ugly and stupid. My new stepfather would test me on oral maths. I never got one sum right. My mother sent me to an Educational Psychologist. She kept the report for 70 years and recently passed it on to me, and I keep it with some old photos of that time

Me and Little Robot

<u>THIS REPORT IS PRIVATE AND CONFIDENTIAL.</u>

Nicolette Sinclair Loutit was tested with the most recent revision of the Stanford-Binet Scale of Intelligence Tests on Feb. 12nd 19§§.   At that time her age was 7 years and 8 months and her mental age, according to the tests passed, was 9 years and 4 months.   This gives her an Intelligence Quotient of 122.   Owing to tha nature of some of her failures it is probable that this result somewhat underestimates her actual ability but, in any case, the fact is established that she has dscidedly superior mental ability when related to the population as a whole,

although not more than approximates the high average found in schools which give the more advanced types of education.

During the test Nicolette worked with steady purpose, although she h̶a̶ isual memory for ⸳

I was facinated by my mothers paints at a very young age.

In my work room, I have a little table my mother used for years in her studio in Spain. I find the stains beautiful.

I returned into one of my favorite cowboy games

MY BIKE ARRIVED. I WAS HAPPY. I learnt to
skid on it. I played with the older boys. I loved Tim, &
Charles. We made camps in the wood. We smoked
hollowed out cow parsley stalks. I loved sleeping in
dormitories. I slowly learnt to read, and write badly.
I painted happily. I enjoyed country dancing and
Eurythmics too – wich I discovered was considered
ridiculous- outside school. The macgibbon family came
to some of my 'sports days'. I felt part of the
school. Best of all was going to assembly twice a
term at the big school. At the begining of term
the hymn 'Oh God our help in ages Past' was
sung. I loved the deep male voices. I'd sit cross
legged on the floor in the front row, silent
and entranced.

   I dreaded the holidays, but pretended not
to. I suffered terrible boils at 'home' and school.
They had to be squeezed & bandaged.
Worst of all were the slow painful injections,
done with a thick needle.

I still have the scars of the boils (and more in many places)

But one scar that puzzels me more, was why I ran away. One day someone called one an 'Aborigeni'. We were propably learning about them, and I was aware my nose was considered big ~too big~ like 'them'......

It was said as an insult, I felt obliged to be insulted and run off. So, I did. I ran away. I was running away, & had no idea where too.

It was raining

I PUT ON MY BOOTS and Garberdene raincoat...

I didn't talk about my home, my two step fathers, — the possible things I could be running away from — but school wasn't one of them.

I loved running away.

I'm still running away

perhaps I better go back

and hide in the ROHDODENDRONS

NICOLEEETTE NICOLEE

← RHODODENDRONS →

SCHOOL DRIVE

I loved Mr Cooper, he was kind and cared for me. Mrs cooper & I disliked each other. She taught us 'the facts of life', a drew images that still haunt me.

STICK PEOPLE WITH HOLES O or BITS. — BIT MAN ONTOP OF HOLE MAN

But the scar — the last one at that school was my cowardice

She's not happy at that school

New headmistress

No she doesn't like all those rough BOYS — much nicer here with our well behaved girls.

you'd like it here, wouldn't you

YES

HELP NO NO NO NO WHATS HAPPENING

I started

in my new school, determined to be a good
~~school~~ school girl. The 1st night I was
told to kneel down by my bed and say
the Lords Prayer. I had no idea what
that meant. I'd not heard of Jesus, Mary,
or even 'God - our <u>father</u>.' At least I'd
heard 'O God our help in ages past' sung
at the senior school of my previous
school, so I was aware I must learn
of something very important and powerful
and I did.

I was 10, I'd lost Mr Cooper. I'd lost my friends, and begun to be a good little prep school girl, ~~amidst a~~ Controlled by a group of mostly disturbed 'teachers'. Home too was complicated and always changing — (my second sister was born, I loved her, but saw her rarely.)

Only 10 and the assaults began, where ever I was.

Being a good little prepschool girl didn't last more than a year.

The headmistress taught me painting and clay modeling. I understood her teaching.

LOOK LOOK

DO IT

FEEL IT!

Her husband 'TC' taught us Latin & Divinity.

EVEN I COULD DO LATIN as he drew everything.

YES NO — PUELLA NAUTA!

HORSE

EQU

'DIVINITY' LESSONS Usually from HIS BED

Often TC would be unwell with his weak heart. I loved going upstairs to his bedroom.

Sometimes we, the favorites, were invited to visit TC at night in his bedroom.

It was a spookey Elizabethan House

Old, dark, creaking

Occasionally We would be caught

GET BACK TO YOUR BEDS IMMEDIATLY

His matress was high up on an old Bath

Images from Under Milk Wood became
vivid. Images of the trees outside his window
became God filled in our talk. We'd be
snug in his bed ~ exploring life itself,
in a way new to me ~ God was in my
head and my understanding'. Bible
Black night ~ milk chocolate ~ & the smell
of flannel pyjamas ~ HIS pyjamas covering
his frail white body.

If his heart was hurting he'd ask me
to put my head on his heart
'LOUTIT LOUTIT LAY YOUR
HEAD ON MY
HEART.'

FLY INTO THE SEA—GOON...

Just to divert — my diversion swimming or fantasy swimming, is a way to find quietness. Its similar to my Zen meditation (which I've done intensely, but ran from a few years ago, well not it but the monk hierachy and institutnalization.) It's a dive into that quietness within me, and being as aware as I dare of the without.

In the christmas Holidays I met my father again after a few years. He was persauded by James MacGibbon to take me on a sailing trip across the channel, and his son Robert — my friend was coming too. James, Robert & I caught the train to Portsmoth, it was dark & we went to the restaurant car. I was very happy, and we all had tea & welsh Rabbit — I can smell it now, and the train so cosy and the dark outside, & safe with the MacGibbons.

We set off for France ~ James, Robert, my father
and I ~ It was dark
and raining, a smell of wet grass, thick ropes
and the salty sea. The boat had to get
through a lock to catch the tide to
take us out to sea. Whilst the boat
was ~~down~~ low in the dark pit of water, a
man fell down between the boat and
the side of the lock wall, & drowned......

[A month ago my friend 'little Robert' told me
the man ~~did~~ did not die.]

'Bedtime' I was put in the fo'c's'le in a hammock style bunk.
you're special like your mother
I'm only doing this because I love your mother
does this feel nice?
NO NO NO
NO NO
BUT THIS FEELS NICE. Doesn't it?
yes yes yes
No No No

And into the storm

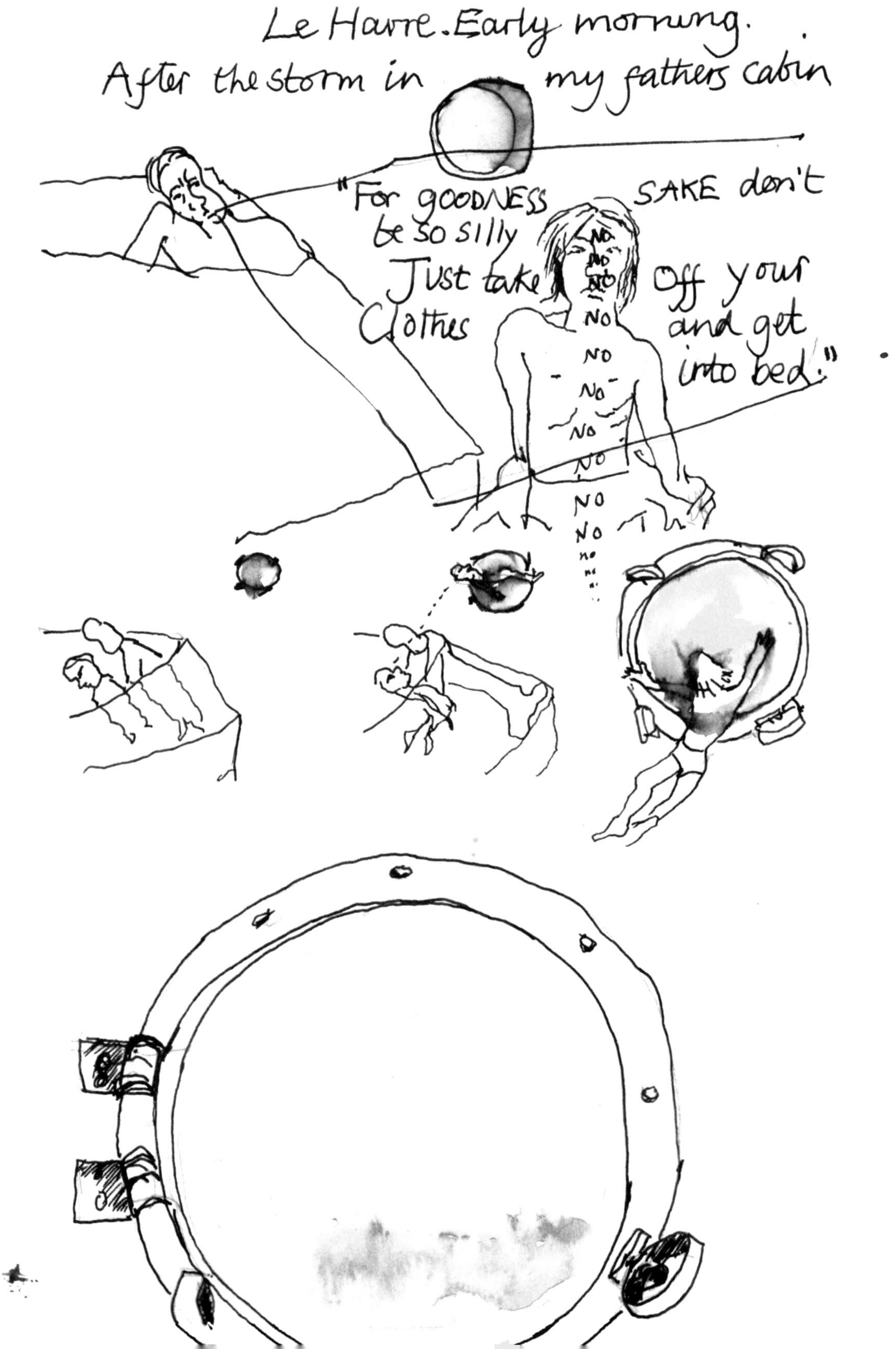
Le Havre. Early morning.
After the storm in my fathers cabin
"For GOODNESS SAKE don't be so silly Just take Off your Clothes and get into bed."
NO NO NO NO NO NO NO NO NO NO no no no

It took us a week
I remember little
It was cold.

to PARIS

carried us all the same

The beautiful boat

ICED FEAR

A CRUEL JOURNEY

NO, I remember the warmth in a barges Cabin

I remember Lonlyness and the smell of damp wood & bed sheets

I remember the shock of Pans loud and fast & dark.

And Now

Now

NOW

NOW

Now — Colours on my window sill.

Now,

I remember — a link.

(~~and~~ 66 years ago

ROBERT well done NICKY

I love colouring in

PARIS CAFÉ

Thick wax crayons that could barely colour

As a child most colours drew me into a state of quiet smoothness — colours and images. I loved colouring in, though I preferred my own shapes.

At Hamspray at breakfast time — quiet and a little tense — usually just me, Ralph with his pink financial times and Frances with her letters — I'd look at Carringtons painting of 'the Mill at tidemarsh' — green water reflecting the sky. I'd hold that image in my head, or body. If things were hard I'd remember a print of a waterfall, in the passage upstairs.

At my prepschool there was a painting in the hall where we ate and gathered, by William Coldstream of a bridge pale ochre, and green water flowing underneath. I gazed into it for hours one afternoon when I had to stay behind and finish my Irish stew. I sat in a green flow with the grizzel in my cheek.

As an adult I've returned to some of those images and I'm disappointed that my visual memory isn't at all accurate. I stored recreated colours and filled images my way.

Sometimes, colours had a distressing effect, but mostly they comfort. My house is hand painted in colours that move me. Our home is a giant colouring in book.

 These 3 colours of those wax crayons nauseate me, facinate me. They introduced me to my interior world that saved me. I met them in Paris, during my 1st visit.

and during the 2nd trip to Paris I could escape, I was learning the depths of our minds, other times it was not so.

No, memory doesn't always appear in whole images.

To be back at my prep school was a relief.
In the summer, we were free – in the long afternoons
to play outside – walking to the woods, climbing
trees – fighting on the grass, and the 'good girls'
played tennis or rode their ponies. I was strong, &
like most of us a 'tomboy'. We weren't embaressed
by our bodies, or particularly modest. Sometimes
we were allowed to swim in the large lily pond,
we had to get undressed in our dorms, &
run naked – running was compulsoary, up
the drive – past the cedar tree, the chapel on
the hill & then into the pool, where 2
teachers were 'in charge' sitting, hen like, on the
edge.
One terrible summer afternoon ------

PLEASE GO IMMEDIATELY AND COVER YOURSELF UP

BLAND
BLACK REJECTION.

My last year at that school ~~were~~ was
Sad and baffeling.
Extraordinarily – 60 years later – a month ago –
One of my best friends from that time

Contacted me. She's living in America.
I'd admired her at school for being very clever
and quiet & clear. I was sad when she left
a year before me to go back to America. She
gave me all the letters I wrote to her during
my last year. Here's part of one:

The people in the row behind us where
making very embarissing remarks about
what dreary !clothes he wore, quite
True I suppose.
I loathe This Term since yesterday
because I had a ghastly blowing
up, by Mr Sharp, I never knew
why, nor did I ever know
Mr Sharp could be so beastly
He told me "I think
you are a horrible child
I and all the Staff are
very glad you are leaving,
because of This and That
And oh! he made me so Miserble
and lonley, But Why? I have
been Trying to be good, And have
been, I know I. haven't been rude
or anything Why? Why? oh! I loathe
him and he knows it.
You probably think I'm a pool
and This is all untrue but
Its not, Its to like a very
unjust Nightmare, He must have
been eavesdropping when I said
something about him. But then he
has, no right to blows me up
But I wont go on about all my troubles
xxxxxx Goodbye honey bun, darling, oh Gee
Nickes

Major Sharp he had the same rage as my 1st step father Robert
NICOLETTE SURELY YOU CAN ADD 10 + 7
1 2 3 4 5 6 7 8
NO UMM NO UMMMM
TOO MANY BLOBS TO COUNT
THWACK
Was he a War Hero?
He marched in his shiney shoes
I still can't add 10 + 7, not really

So I acted strong.

So I acted strong.

STILL DO

I still hear the
headmistresses voice
when I paint

I still remember
the english teacher
who liked me. She had
beautyful dark eyes, & wore a leather
jerkin. When she asked me out
to tea I refused. I still long
to have tea with her.

(In revenge when I was grown up, I mildly
seduced a priest in his black smelly robe.)

One of the reasons why abused people
don't 'report it', is that they cant
articulate it. Words dont
do. Its complex this
articulation

Yes

thus articulated truck arrives in
my heart.

A Soundless
Wham

& like a 6 year
old the image making
undoes the brutality.

articulated
truck going sung gone?

seals
moaning their
song

LUST FOR LIFE

where's that
giotto angel
lady?

then there's mothers
and [mothers] too

ran away   went
                  wild   kept to
                            herself
         gran   mother
Gt Gran

That's another story.

Me and Noa
No one told me what old age was like
?
So tell me
Then what do I need to know?
I don't know what to say
AIEEE....
well....
Blah Blah. I want to be kind and things hurt more & give me joy more and I care more & less and blah blah
Too much to explain

And that's why I'm doing this.

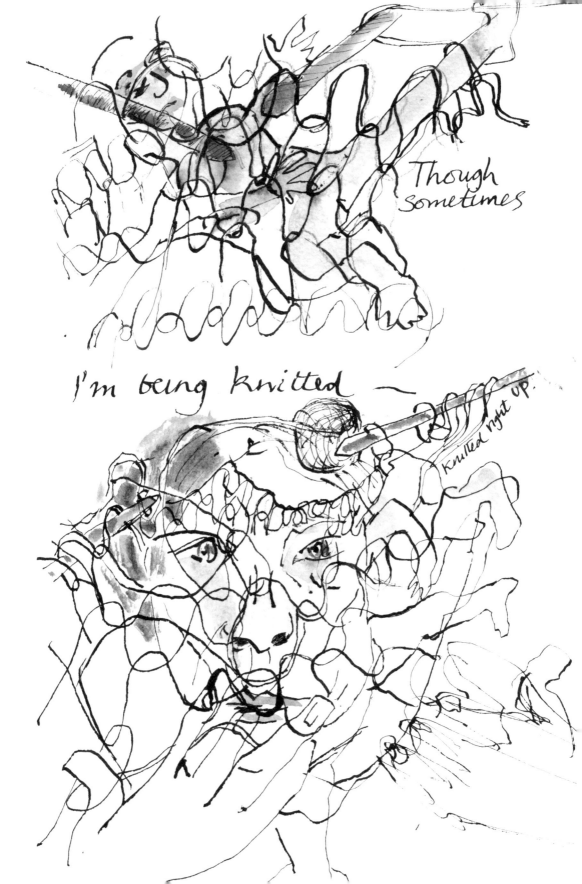

Though
sometimes

I'm being knitted —

knitted right up.

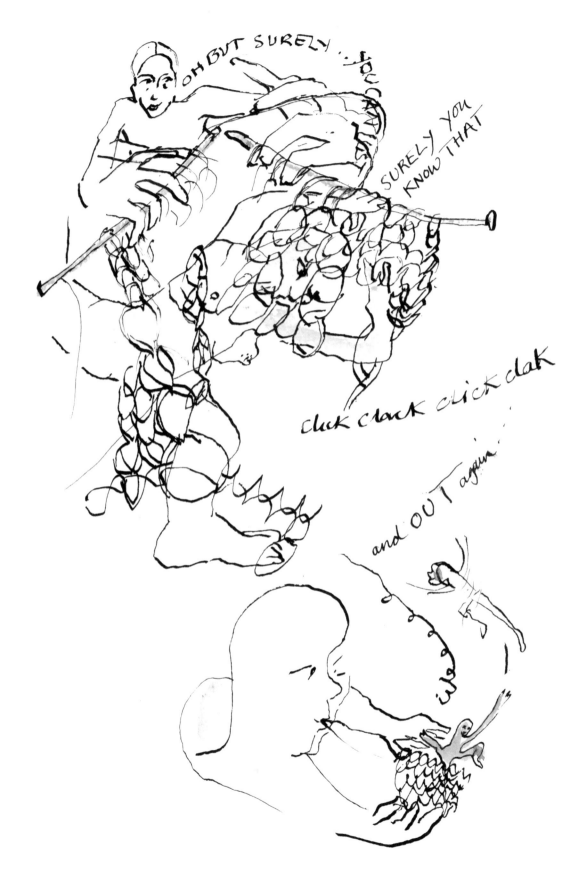

As I get older, wonderful things
happen too. I had a cataract out,
light floods in

End of February.

Vision without a lense in my eye
During the operation.

NO GLASSES
'spectacles'
Gone

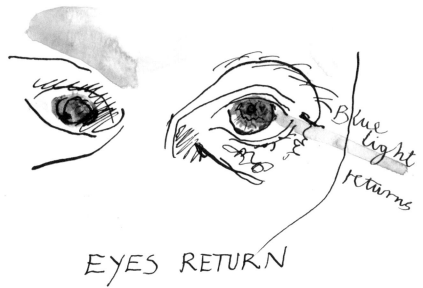

Blue
light
returns

EYES RETURN

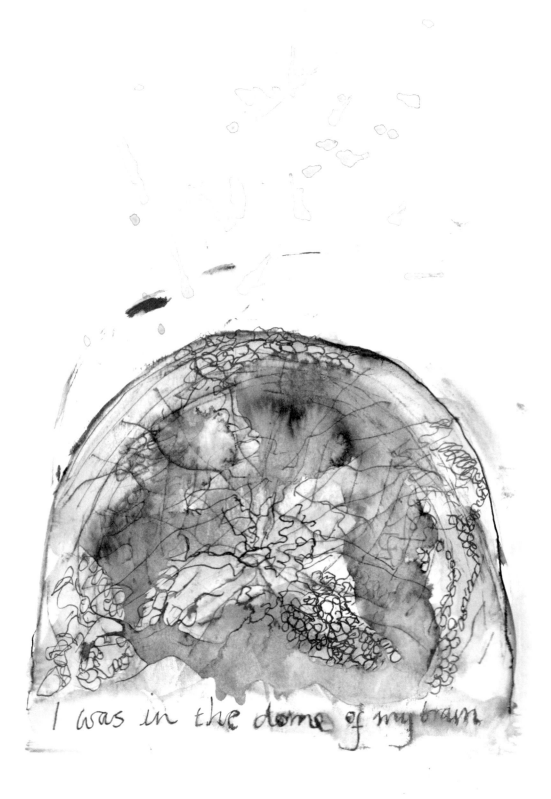

I was in the dome of my brain.

Next morning, the sun rises, I just catch it.

walk out to the sea to hawk and not think

But,
Have I let my roots go numb?

Have I lost my base?

Whilst doing this book, going for walks — choosing which type — sea, marsh, the angels tump, the cuthberts field has given me strength and comfort, but increasingly my feet have become numb ("quite common in old age") my balance wobbley, and thighs weak. I've been trying not to complain — and failing.

I'm a blob

I must place my slippers

smile — I have — I still have 2 feet

and I'm so flexible

The G.P. referred me for a 2nd visit to the Neurologist
"and did those feet in ancient times WALK upon englands green and pleasant land"
LaLaLa Lahhhh
Not sure.. yes.. no yes NO
can you feel this
OR THIS
I'm worried its getting WORSE
"PERIPHIAL NEUROPATHY"
NO ITS NO WORSE
BUT MY Thighs are weaker too
NO YOUR Thighs arn't Weak.
I LOVE AUTUMN

Walking in the cuthberts field yesterday I
noticed that I felt strangely strong. My thighs
-my 'weak thighs' were doing the walking -
stout active little pegs. My feet were still
numb, but more 'like enclosed in extra shoes
-less flipper like. As I walked I was wanting
to add more to this story, though it's over,
I felt there could be a ∃ profound finale.

An After word
name names -explain look- consider-

My thigh is strong

STRONG   ON WE GO

"and did those feet
in ancient times
walk upon Englands -
green and pleasant
LAND"

And Then I fell over.

I saw hares playing

Heard a bird singing

It was fine I felt happy with my face in the grass

In the grass I remembered play-fighting with my friend Bimba Macniece who I haven't thought of for years.

And of course
my dog Neddy
took it all in.